Princess Eliza

Villa Cimbrone, Ravello

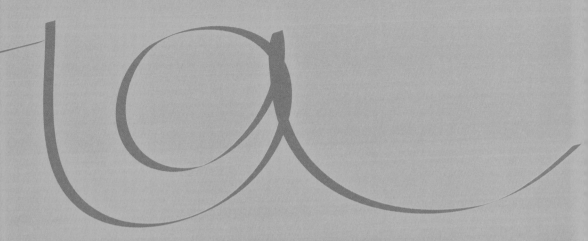

Italian Joy Carla Coulson

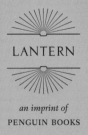

LANTERN

an imprint of
PENGUIN BOOKS

To the Italians, who opened their doors and their hearts, and taught me a new way of living, eating and loving.

To my mum and dad, who showed me what love is — for always knowing when to hold me close and when to let me go.

And for Popi: She's small and petite, and at seventy-four years of age she's still beautiful. Her hands mesmerise you when she speaks; it's a love story between a conductor and an orchestra — they dip, ebb, pause and gesticulate wildly in circles. Her eyes hold the freshness and excitement of a sixteen-year-old. She fits underneath your arm and has the nose of a princess . . . she was born Tamara Zazzeri but to everyone who loves her, she will always be Popi.

Introduzione 1

contents

There will a
when you
Everything
That
the beg

ome a time

believe

s finished.

will be

Louis L'Amour

inning.

Italy has always held a place in my heart.

introduzione

introduction

Florence

I had it all. Well, that's what everybody told me. A small Art Deco apartment in Darlinghurst, Sydney, filled with beautiful objects: a Murano chandelier from Venice (Italy), a handmade vase from Bahia (Brazil), chairs from Copenhagen (Denmark) and rugs handmade in Rajasthan (India). My wardrobe was overflowing with beaded silk dresses by Collette Dinnigan, ruched leather stilettos by Gucci and clothes that looked more like art by Akira. Fresh flowers were delivered on Mondays; and on Tuesdays the cleaner let herself in and put my 55 square metres back into perfect order, leaving my washing neatly folded and ironed on my bed. My successful business of thirteen years afforded me trips to exotic locations around the world to collect even more beautiful possessions for my home.

Sounds good on paper, but in reality I felt like just another invisible female fast approaching my use-by date in a city that worships youth. My male peers were dating girls who were celebrating their twenty-first birthday, and the hope that Mr Right would save me from the burden of doing it all on my own was fading. I was a 35-year-old woman still taking the rubbish out on my own, changing my own light bulbs, paying my own mortgage and arriving at family functions without the 'family'. My weekends were kept busy with endless shopping trips to fill my already overflowing wardrobe and the void that would have been satisfied

by love. As I arrived home from work late at night, I began to dread the
idea of entering my empty apartment with just an answering machine full
of messages and Thai takeaway for one.

Christmas 2000 was almost upon us, and one by one my single friends
were pairing up and moving on. While their letterboxes were filling with
Christmas cards from Barbeques Galore and Babyco, mine was filling
with takeaway menus. If food equals love, I'd deduced that my soul was
dead: takeaway coffee in cardboard cups and soulless dinners for one
prepared by nameless chefs in nondescript restaurants. The closest I had
come to any kind of relationship of late was with my local Thai delivery boy,
who knew me by order: Ms Tofu stir-fry and vegetables (hold the oil).

As the levels of joy in everyone around me soared as Christmas neared,
mine were plummeting. The idea of fronting up to yet another family Christmas
alone, and a New Year on the way that looked like being the same as the one
that was almost over were just painful reminders of what my life hadn't become.
As I opened my Thai takeaway on Christmas Eve, there among the plastic was
a small wrapped gift. As the most valued client of my local Thai takeaway, I had
been given a silver jewellery box and a 2001 laminated takeaway menu for my
fridge. I was mortified; I had never felt so lost and lonely.

There's a turning point in everyone's life, and that silver jewellery
box was mine. It was a reminder that life was passing me by. Every late
night, every failed relationship, every childhood dream of what life would be
and the fear that the woman inside me was slowly dying was magnified by
that Christmas gift sitting on my coffee table staring back at me. I realised
in that moment that I could stay living a life that looked good only from the
outside, or break out and find what it was in life I was searching for. Images
of meetings with middle-aged marketing managers danced before my eyes,

and the concept of another thirteen years in small, grey city offices seemed inconceivable. It was over. My friends cheered me on when I rented out my apartment, put my life in storage, sold my business, packed two suitcases and my second-hand Nikon and headed for Italy.

Italy has always held a place in my heart, since my days as a backpacking twenty-year-old. I will never forget the feeling of awe as I exited the train station at Venice and clapped my eyes on the Grand Canal and the faded *palazzi* (palaces), with the musical Italian language surrounding me. Or the image of thousands of flickering candles held towards the sky at the encore of the opera *Aida* in the ancient Roman theatre in Verona. To me, over the years it was only natural to return and pass holidays in Florence, Rome and Venice, listening to that language I always dreamed of learning.

Italy was to be my first port of call but ended up my final destination. After years of being weighed down by possessions, I'd thought long and hard about what was important to me out of all the beautiful objects I had accumulated. It was easy: the photographs stuck to my fridge; nieces, nephews, birthdays, laughter, tears, parties, weddings, graduations and the emotions of life captured forever. They were the only objects I unpacked when I arrived at Popi's house in Florence.

I met Popi while I was searching for an apartment. It was August and Florence was unbearably hot. My Italian-language classmate, Piotr, extolled the virtues of a woman named Popi, who for twenty-five years had opened her house to students from around the world. Piotr told me he was living in a house 'like paradise' with five other students, and encouraged me to

move in. Being a one-bedroom-apartment girl, I seriously doubted my abilities to cohabit with that many.

I soon discovered, however, that Popi was everything Piotr said; an eccentric Italian *mamma* filled to the brim with Mediterranean fervour and generosity. I came to love pushing open her front door at the end of each day to be greeted by the scents of cooking, like I did all those years ago when I was just a skinny teenager growing up in Mudgee, New South Wales. I began to meander through the medieval streets between *il duomo* (the cathedral) and Piazza Beccaria on my way home, each day discovering something new. When I needed a little more open space, I would follow the course of the river Arno from the Ponte Vecchio, passing Ponte alle Grazie and Ponte di San Niccolò as I watched the rowers practise on the river.

I enrolled in a photography course and practised my Italian at home every morning over coffee and brioche, the light streaming into the kitchen from the *terrazzo* (terrace). I paid two weeks' rent in advance and stayed for two years.

Florence became my playground, Piazza della Signoria and the *Fontana di Nettuno* (Fountain of Neptune) as familiar as Bondi Beach and its rolling waves. Cellini's *Perseo* (Perseus), proudly holding the head of Medusa, winked at me as I made my way home at night. The spontaneity of Italian life seduced me. Nothing was planned ahead, it just happened; *aperitivi* (drinks) with friends, summer evenings listening to string quartets in the *piazza* (square) and sojourns to Naples, Venice, Positano or wherever the whim or Trenitalia (the Italian rail system) would take me.

I dreamed I was Annie Leibovitz by day and Audrey Hepburn by night. To me, Sydney became merely the name of a great actor from the 1960s. Life was simple and lived at a new pace. I bought a bicycle (with a

I dreamed I was Annie Leibovitz by day and Audrey Hepburn by night.

small basket attached) for transport, I took *la passeggiata* (evening strolls)
through Florence's ancient city streets at night and enjoyed endless dinners
and conversation wrapped together under the soft light that illuminated
Popi's table. Each day became an adventure, ordering a *spremuta d'arancia*
(fresh orange juice) or a *tramezzino* (sandwich) a challenge. Going to school
again after all those years of working in an office was exhilarating. Almost
anything felt possible.

The first year passed slowly. I savoured the sunshine on my back, the
afternoon music along the Arno, the heavenly food that Popi prepared every
night and the myriad handsome men that called '*Ciao bella!*' or offered
me a *caffè* (coffee) as I walked by.

I traded my second-hand Nikon for my pride and joy: a robust black
Leica (the Manolo Blahnik of cameras). My sojourns to Naples, Positano and
Venice became photo stories and I had found my calling. My camera opened
up a life about which I had only ever fantasised; a life filled with people,
excitement, passion and exuberant discussions without an end.

At times I couldn't help but wonder who I thought I was to become
a photographer in a strange country, with a new language and without any
help. I went to London and knocked on the doors of as many magazines as
possible; I took the train to Milan overcome with nervous anxiety at the
thought of selling myself in Italian; and I canvassed Australian magazines
when I was home at Christmas. Then, one day, a single, slow tear slid down
my cheek when I read that first email from *Marie Claire* magazine with the
magic words — 'We like it' — and the dream I had held back all those years
started to come true. Slowly, my photos and stories were published, and
photography became not only my passion but my career. I photographed
people, places, fashion and life.

There's a time and place for everything in life, and after two years and eight 'seasons' of the finest food I have ever eaten, the time came to create the next part of my life. Popi didn't say goodbye, just '*A presto*' (See you soon), and she refused to take back the keys to her front door. '*Casa mia è casa tua; vieni quando vuoi*' (My house is your house; come whenever you want) were her parting words.

I found a small apartment on Via Maggio in the heart of Oltrarno (*Oltrarno* literally means 'over the Arno river'), between Piazza Santo Spirito and Palazzo Pitti. I knew the minute I put the key in the door that this would be my new home. Like most of the buildings on Via Maggio, mine was built in the sixteenth century, and climbing the stairs was a better workout than any aerobics class could offer. My apartment is one giant room with a beautiful exposed wooden-beam ceiling, and it came furnished in Florentine style. There is no minimalist designer furniture or avant-garde art, but I love it just the same. My large bed is covered in white (the original Florentine Medusa faces had to go); I have a pull-out sofa (for my friends who come and stay) and a big wooden Tuscan table surrounded by six chairs thatched with straw. The fake Botticellis came down and the all-white walls became the perfect backdrop for a giant collage of my favourite photos and faces.

A soft light infuses my apartment and the window looks out into a *cortile* (courtyard) and into the lives of my neighbours. When I first moved in and one of my neighbours would call across the *cortile* to my neighbour Marco, and Marco would stick his head out the window and engage in an hour-long conversation, I felt like I was intruding into their lives. Now, the chatter, the scents of the evening meal and the occasional over-the-top scene of an angry woman hurling her cheating husband's clothes from the second

floor on to bikes and clothes drying below, screaming, `*Sporco bastardo!*`
(Dirty bastard!) have become part of my life in Italy.

Since the day I left Sydney and my comfortable life, many things have
changed. I'm up the back of the bus more often than the front of the plane.
Paying the rent has become a challenge instead of an Internet transfer.
Time has a new meaning, and words such as `speed dial`, `takeaway` and
`mortgage` are from someone else's language. And that woman who was
dying inside is alive and well, living a rich tapestry of moments and emotions
she always expected and hoped life could be.

Venice

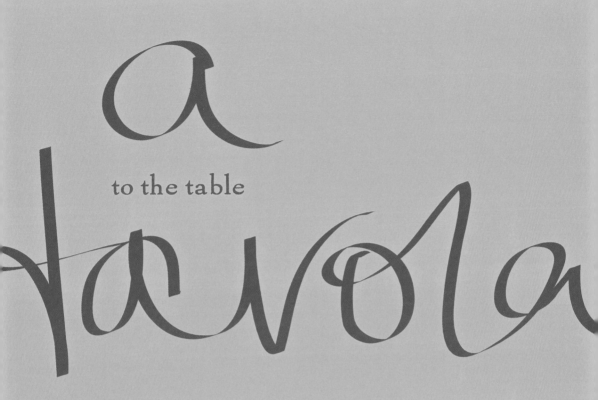

a
to the table
tavola

The house was enormous; a double-storeyed villa that dominated the corner of two busy streets just a stone's throw from Ponte di San Niccolò and the river Arno. Faded Tuscan yellow filled my vision, punctuated only by the deep-green shutters that swing from every Florentine home and the brightly coloured geraniums sitting high atop the *terrazzi* (terraces). Enormous wooden doors towered above my head and butterflies fluttered in my stomach as I stood with my finger poised on the doorbell of Signora Popi Zazzeri. The August sun seared into my shoulders and I secretly cursed Piotr, the Swiss student from my Italian-language class who had given me Popi's number. It seemed like a very bad idea at the ripe old age of thirty-five to be going to live with an Italian woman who was older than my mother and with students who I imagined would be the age of my young cousins. I had exhausted all avenues of finding an apartment or even a room in Florence as the city slowly shut down for the August holiday. The renovation above the small *pensione* (boarding house) where I was staying in Piazza Santo Stefano seemed like the only activity left in the city, and between the noise and the heat I was frazzled. It didn't matter how many phone calls I made or how many apartments I saw; there was always a hitch. 'Signorina, we are sorry, but to get to the bathroom we must pass through your room,' or 'We are looking for someone who doesn't mind vacating the room on Wednesdays and Fridays, when our

Eric

Jessica

Pop and Pesto!

father uses it as his doctor's studio. Or like the last apartment I had seen,
which was a little too close to a scene from *The Young Ones* (complete
with an Italian version of Neil sprawled in the lounge room) for my liking.
I decided that Piotr and his *casa come un paradiso* (house like paradise)
was my last option. I pressed the doorbell and jumped ever so slightly as
it automatically sprang open. 'I'll just stay a week,' I reassured myself.

The house was cool and dark and, like a Pied Piper, the smell of
freshly baked *schiacciata* (a delicious 'squashed' bread like a focaccia)
called me up the stairs. Posters of 1960s pop artist Roy Lichtenstein hung
on the walls of the stairwell. A small voice called from the second flight,
'*Buongiorno, cara mia*' (Good morning, my dear). I reached the next
flight and saw a beautiful woman dressed in a bright red caftan, with rings
covering her fingers and a long silver charm necklace tinkling around her
neck. Her toenails were beautifully manicured and painted bright pink.
A tendril of smoke from her cigarette caused her to squint as she dispensed
with a handshake and offered her cheek. '*Sono Popi*,' she said. 'There's
lots of us, I hope you don't mind. We even have someone on the divan,' she
apologised and explained in the same breath.

Popi's house had seven bedrooms, which were always full. My 8m²
room consisted of a single bed (the end of which I could easily touch with my
toes) and a wardrobe that required an Olympic manoeuvre if I wanted to open
it while standing in front of it. A giant magnolia tree and the terracotta roofs
of Florence filled the view from my window.

Breakfast was served at eight and cleared by ten as everyone went off
to school. The aroma of bubbling tomatoes, baked ricotta and *pasta al dente*
floated up the stairs ten hours later; the time it took to create the evening
meal. '*A tavola!*' (which translates literally as 'To the table', but it's the

Photography gave me whatever it was that was missing inside and it made me love life again.

Lungarno, Florence

Italian equivalent of 'Dinner's ready') was the call to dinner, the highlight of the 'family's' day.

The fragrance of crushed basil preceded *a tavola* that first night; pesto was to be our *primo piatto* (first dish). Popi's pesto was a knockout, and Piotr glanced across the table with an I-told-you-so look as I slowly devoured mine. Rich, colourful, sensuous food kept appearing from somewhere beyond the kitchen door. '*Il cameriere è sempre in vacanza*' (The waiter is always on holidays) was the cue to help yourself to it all. Saucepans that had simmered for hours preparing the *secondo piatto* (second dish) of chicken and olives in a tomato *sugo* (sauce), the *contorni* (side dishes of vegetables) of Tuscan *fagioli* (white beans) soaked in olive oil, *spinaci* (spinach) and *patate* (potatoes) flavoured with rosemary arrived one after the other. '*Vuoi ancora?*' (Would you like more?) was Popi's mantra, asked before the last mouthful had melted in your mouth.

That first night passed quickly under the soft light suspended above Popi's table. Seated around it were: Eric, an American Ivy League student studying Italian literature; Paola, a Mexican jeweller searching for new inspiration; Philippa, a Swiss exhibition designer at the Musées d'art et d'histoire in Geneva; Lilian, a diplomat's wife from Guatemala, who was studying Italian; Piotr (my Italian-language classmate), a Swiss student of medicine; and Alessandra, a German *sigggnnora* who translated French and English. They discussed topics I had never heard about, places I had always dreamed of going and, one by one, all of the varying passions that guided their lives. Not one of my new housemates had the same passport but they all had one thing in common: they had chosen what they loved in life as a career.

That table and the opportunities it brought seemed endless. For me, Popi was everything in my life that Sydney wasn't. Countless summer nights

passed with the scent of gardenias in the air and the roar of Vespas below.
The constant array of new and familiar faces all shared stories while Popi
distributed her own kind of love — food. My dreams, projects and horizons
grew. I began to live.

I enrolled in a photography course and bought a bicycle that had seen
better days. I began practising my Italian with Cesarina (one of the many
members of Popi's extended family) and Popi, while they blanched tomatoes
and diced onions for the evening's minestrone. I tortured them with my
Italian, and the corner chair became my chair. I was seduced by the morning
preparation that is fundamental to an Italian kitchen and the evening meal.
The aroma of *aglio* (garlic) hitting *olio d'oliva* (olive oil) in the pan and
sautéing onions scented the air while Popi and Cesarina peeled purple-green
artichokes and baked polenta. I continued my tirade of questions about what
they were preparing and why it tasted so good. The most important thing,
they explained, was to take time to 'put love into the food; never hurry and it
will always taste good.' As the 'family' tumbled down the stairs for breakfast,
they always gravitated towards the kitchen with its melody of laughter,
singing and cooking. As we made our way to school, the doorbell usually rang,
bringing with it members of Popi's family, whose faces soon became familiar.

If my school hours allowed, I begged Popi to let me go with her to do
the shopping at Mercato di Sant'Ambrogio. I loved the atmosphere of the
market, where Popi tucked her arm through mine as we wove our way in and
out of the stalls selecting the finest produce. Bruno from the butcher always
saved the finest cut of lamb for her; Luigi wrapped the *marzolino* (a soft
pecorino cheese made from sheep's milk, traditionally served in the spring
month of *marzo* (March), hence its name) in white waxed paper decorated
with small baskets; and Antonella fussed over us as she put the fresh

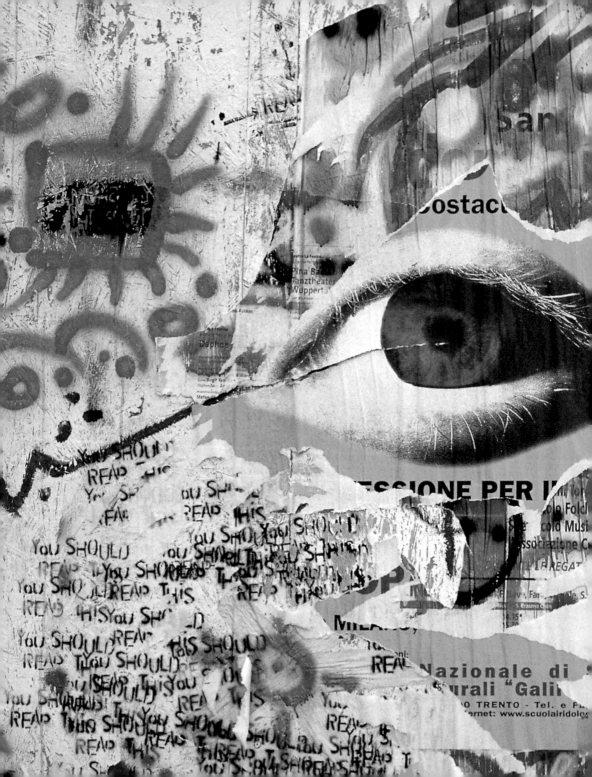

rocket and lettuce into brown paper bags. When we finished shopping, and whenever the corner booth at Cibreo Caffè was still free, we would stop in for a cappuccino and a warm brioche and watch *le signore* (the ladies) sugaring their coffee at the small wooden tables.

Returning to school and studying something I had always adored was a gift, but studying it in Italian proved a lot more difficult than I could ever have imagined. My *professore* (professor) was as passionate about photography as his students. He carried a 1950s Rolleiflex around in his bag and was often seen at lunchtime shooting, yet again, the spires of Santa Croce. We spent hours poring over the images of Jeanloup Sieff, Henri Cartier-Bresson, Jan Saudek and Robert Capa, entering their world each afternoon and not wanting to leave. '*Hai capito?*' (Do you understand?) my teacher barked at me whenever my eyes glazed over, not understanding a word he had said. He would quickly explain the concept again in his pidgin English, but most times I was still none the wiser. More than once I left school with tears streaming down my face, wondering if I would ever get it. I am sure he did, too.

After all those years of running a business, juggling a thousand things at once and arriving home exhausted, I felt exhilarated to be able to attend school and that my homework was to take photos. The first time an image of a little girl laughing appeared between my hands in the darkroom I was hooked. There wasn't a time of day or night that I didn't carry my camera with me and shoot the subtleties of Italian life: granita stalls selling sugared lemon ice in Naples; Vespas flying by with a family of three crammed on; ornate fountains in Rome; couples dancing in the afternoon light along the Arno; *i baristi* (barmen) at Rivoire and Paskowski and all the personalities that

inhabit the markets. I photographed *napoletani* (Neapolitans) as they dragged television sets on to the streets and huddled together to watch the World Cup armed with *panini* (rolls), cold beers and remote controls. I shared the pure joy they experienced when Italy kicked a goal, leading them to burst into song, hugging and dancing together, lost in the moment. I entered *trattoria* kitchens and asked to take photos of the chefs and their spaghetti. I entered *botteghe* (workshops) and, among the scent of shaved wood, I watched artisans repair ancient statues or shape iron into ornate gates. I went to the train station first thing in the morning when the ice was still on the ground, and I rode around on my bike in the late afternoon sun catching shadows and silhouettes. I photographed the statues in Piazza della Signoria, shooting *Perseo* (Perseus) and *Nettuno* (Neptune) over and over and over again. Every day was different; the light, the time, the shadows, and I couldn't resist.

When I returned home on freezing winter mornings chilled to the bone, Popi and Cesarina fussed over me with cups of hot chocolate and bowls of steaming soup, insisting '*Ti fa bene!*' (It's good for you!) I fell in love with Italy, with Popi and her mad house, with its heavenly aromas; and I fell in love with photography. Photography gave me a reason to start a conversation or enter someone's life, if only for a moment. It allowed me to reflect on my world and the small things in it that give me great pleasure. It brought me people, places and situations that I hadn't even dared to dream about. Photography gave me whatever it was that was missing inside and it made me love life again.

Singing angel detail, Duomo - Florence

amore love

Roses, Florence

At first glance Italy seemed to me to be one long love scene.

When I first arrived in Italy I was dumbstruck by the number of people, old and young, kissing, hugging, holding and loving each other in public. Church stairs, lamp-lit streets, ancient bridges and *piazze* (squares) would fill with unending displays of public affection. At times I couldn't help but turn away with embarrassment, or sometimes I would have the reverse impulse and stare just a little too long at the scenes before me.

As spring burst over the hills of Tuscany, scenting the air with magnolia, a young couple would lock lips with the passion of those who had never kissed before, not seeing, feeling or hearing the street sweepers and midday shoppers around them. A middle-aged couple entwined in a passionate embrace on *binario 11* (platform 11) would, *Casablanca*-style, unwillingly pull themselves apart as the conductor blew his whistle. In the depths of winter, two *ragazzi* (teenagers) would think nothing of showering each other with tender *baci* (kisses) on the stairs of Santa Croce as a straggle of tourists passed by.

My Anglo-Saxon upbringing had almost forbidden this kind of amorous behaviour in public, so at first glance Italy seemed to me to be one long love scene. The air is charged with *amore* (love), something akin to always having spring in the air.

Fifties Italian cinema idols Vittorio Gassman, Alberto Sordi and Vittorio De Sica all come alive as I pass the *ortolano* (greengrocer), the

legatoria (bookbinder) and the *biciclettaio* (bicycle-repair shop). Their
modern-day counterparts, all actors patiently waiting in the wings for their
moment in the spotlight, are in the meantime content to charm, amuse and
seduce any woman who crosses their path. '*Bellezza in bicicletta!*' (Beauty
on a bike!) escapes from the mouth of Marco as he stacks ripe peaches,
stopping to admire a beautiful girl as she passes by. Paolo leans nonchalantly
on the door, resting a cigarette in his mouth and uttering in a low voice,
'*Complimenti alla tua mamma*' (Compliments to your mother) while the
books he is supposed to be restoring wait in the background. And on those
long winter days when beautiful women are scarce and a gorgeous girl brings
her bicycle in with a flat tyre, showering Carmelo with a smile, he glances
skywards and clasps his hands dramatically together, exclaiming, '*C'è un
dio!*' (There is a god!)

   Italian men love the chase, the romance, the game, the titillation,
the excitement and, above all, they love women. In Italy, sexual tension
sparks and everyone openly flirts. Italian men, unlike their Anglo-Saxon
counterparts, don't give up if a woman says no. To an Italian man, a refusal
isn't a put-down or a reason to give up; it's a challenge and makes the chase
all the more interesting. They are self-confident and believe that eventually
it will be impossible for *le signorine* (the girls) to resist their charms — and
a large percentage of the time they are right!

   I remember the first Italian I dated: Salvatore, a 'young man of the
sea' who sailed ancient wooden boats between Capri and a small beach on
the Amalfi Coast. When Salvatore told me he lived with his mother
I couldn't help releasing a giggle. I moved out of my parents' house (like
most other Australian teenagers in a hurry to get on with growing up)
and commenced paying rent at the grand old age of nineteen. One of the

Streets of passion

Heart

ponte santa trinita

books of love

Santa Croce

just married

Trulli, Puglia

images that soothed the pain when Salvatore passed me over for a younger, blonder Dutch-supermodel type was that they would be making love in his childhood bed, muffling their passion while trying not to wake his mother, who slept in the adjoining bedroom. I knew they would never run naked through the house or make love on the couch, because his mother and her extended family were always huddled together in the kitchen stirring giant saucepans of *sugo* (sauce) and sipping black coffee. I have since learned that the majority of Italian men live with their family, and I wouldn't even consider a giggle at the notion these days.

The word 'privacy' doesn't exist in the Italian language. It isn't that they just left it out of their vocabulary; the Italians simply had no reason to use it. In Italy there is no privacy, hence no word. Italians have now adopted the English version, which is pronounced in their Italianised way of emphasising every syllable — 'prii-vaa-cyee'.

This explains all the smooching and canoodling in public. No prii-vaa-cyee at home with *Mamma* and *Nonna* hanging around, so the *piazze* and *strade* (streets) become a much more 'private' place to do your loving. Almost any *piazza* or public space in Italy — whether it's Piazza San Marco in Venice, Campo de' Fiori in Rome, the Ponte Vecchio in Florence or Piazza Plebiscito in Naples — on any given night or day will be home to the myriad lovers getting to know each other. Lingering kisses, long looks, touching and caressing will be on display for any passer-by as the lovers go about their courting in public, whispering to each other, '*Come sei bella*' (You are so beautiful), '*Non c'è nessuno come te*' (There is no one like you) and '*Ti amo*' (I love you).

In love, words don't count; what count

Nell' amo
non cont
conta la

ATTACCO
AUTOPOMPA

the music.

Francesco is my *amore*. For the past two years we have been seen smooching in public while dangling our legs over Ponte Santa Trìnita in Florence on a warm summer's night; eating gelato and soaking up the sun along the rocks in the small fishing village of Giovinazzo where he passed every summer holiday as a child; and kissing under lampposts or stopping on the Ponte Vecchio like all the lovers before and after us have done and will do as though it's the most natural thing in the world. Italy is a wonderful place to be in love, and to Italians love is the most natural of all emotions.

My *amore* is tall, dark and handsome with tiger-coloured (yellow-green) eyes, jet-black hair and a deep, gravelly voice. When he walks around the house in just a white singlet with a cigarette dangling from his lips, Alain Delon and Marcello Mastroianni spring to mind. I feel like we are starring in our own Fellini film, with 'That's amore' on repeat. We are in love.

I remember the first time Francesco said '*Ti amo*' to me, confirming my status as his *amore*. It was my first holiday in the region of Puglia and the first time I met Francesco's family. Francesco comes from Terlizzi, a small village outside of Bari in Italy's south. Our plan was to spend ten days eating, sleeping, swimming and seeing as much of Puglia as we could. Before the touring could start, however, we had an *appuntamento* (date) for lunch at Francesco's parents' house, to meet the family. The house had been dusted and cleaned to within an inch of its life. The best crockery and cutlery, and fresh flowers decorated the table. When we arrived, they were all there: Zia Patrizia, Zia Franca, Zia Maria, Zia Rosa, Zio Franco, Zio Giuseppe, Zia Gina, Zia Nora, *i nonni* (the grandparents), five cousins (whose names I still confuse), Francesco's brother, Beppe, his mother, Chiara, and of course his father, Guiseppe. They had all come to see who had *stregato* (bewitched) their firstborn.

Francesco –

il mio amore

Naples

I had lived in Italy for three years and was convinced I was a seasoned professional at the table. I was mistaken. When it comes to hospitality, southern Italians are the kings. Days are spent preparing a feast. Nothing is forgotten. Bread is baked; zucchinis are roasted and left to soak in olive oil; *panzerotti* are filled with mozzarella and tomato and then fried; *limoncello* is made from the lemons grown on the family farm; and *taralli* (crunchy savoury biscuits) are baked to perfection.

Our feast commenced with the *primo piatto* (first dish) of Francesco's grandmother's handmade orecchiette (little ear-shaped pasta) with tomatoes, rocket and parmesan. Between bites of succulent *burrata Pugliese* (a local cheese that looks like mozzarella but has a filling that melts in your mouth), the questions began. 'Do you have grapes in Australia?' 'Do you have Fiat bambini?' 'Why do you all leave home so young?' 'Can you take the train home or do you have to take the plane?'

By the time the *tiramisù*, *caffè* and *limoncello* were on the table we had eaten eleven different *piatti* and I had lost count of how many questions I had answered. The lunch lasted six hours, and as we headed for the little flat in Giovinazzo where we were staying, I breathed a sigh of relief. Francesco turned to me with those green tiger eyes and said, '*Ti amo.*'

I already felt loved by Francesco, but with those two words he washed away twenty years of disappointment, twenty years of asking myself why I had never found the right person and twenty years of hoping that one day it would happen to me. Unlike English-speakers, Italians do not say 'I love you' to their parents, children or friends; they reserve that melodic phrase — *Ti amo* — for their lover. I knew Francesco would keep those special two words just for me.

I have never had a boyfriend love me in the way Francesco loves me. His tranquil nature brings serenity to everything he does. I feel protected, nurtured and truly cared for by a man for the first time in my life. Francesco has carried the shopping from one end of Florence to the other and up six flights of stairs without being asked. He has walked in the rain to bring me an umbrella when he knew that without it I would be stranded and end up looking like a drowned rat for a dinner he wasn't even going to. He worked for two days straight to buy me the Dolce & Gabbana underwear I saw in the store window one night and uttered, 'When I'm rich that will be the first thing I'll buy.' And he arrived with flowers and *taralli* at the Bari train station when I came to meet his family.

We have shared winter weekends in Venice, our coats pulled around our ears as we drank Martini Bianco in the corner seat at Caffè Florian. We have spent warm summer nights watching re-runs of Bertolucci's *Novecento* in the Roman theatre at Fiesole before racing down the hill back to Florence with the wind in our hair and sunshine in our hearts. We have made love for hours under the covers in the middle of a cold winter's night, shrieking with laughter as a gust of cold air freezes our skin. And Francesco has endured a thirty-one hour plane trip when he couldn't make it through my six-week visit to my family without me, when he had never been on a plane before. All of this, and hearing Francesco's deep, gravelly voice say, '*Grazie a Dio che esisti*' (Thank God you exist)... to me, that's amore.

sexy fountain, Bologna

the market

figs, Florence

lady selling fruit and veg, Spaccanapoli

I push open the heavy wooden door that leads from my apartment to Via Maggio. It's a clear spring morning in Florence, blue skies with just the slightest hint of a cool breeze, and the day is in full flight. *Motorini* (mopeds) fly past, two and three deep, darting in and out of the traffic as they head into *centro* (the centre of town) and over Ponte Santa Trìnita. The sun plays with the *ferro battuto* (wrought iron) that decorates every Florentine window, casting beautiful shadows on the grey cobblestone streets. My first stop is Caffè degli Artigiani in Piazza della Passera, where I am greeted by the laughter and *scherzi* (jokes) of the local artisans who are at the bar. I devour a warm brioche and sip a cappuccino before exiting to the tiny tinkle of the door closing behind me. As I round the corner into Piazza Santo Spirito the bells from Santa Felìcita sound out over Oltrarno, and the morning market hums. Popi teased me a long time ago that I had adopted all the habits of Italians, so, true to her words, like most Italians I can't wait to get to the bar and the market in the morning.

In Piazza Santo Spirito six *bancarelle* (stalls) are manned by Giovanna, Bruno, Giuseppe, Leopoldo, Signora Bianco and Michele. Rain, hail or shine they bring their *pomodori* (tomatoes), *rucola* (rocket), *lattuga* (lettuce), *aglio* (garlic), *cipolle* (onions) and *spinaci* (spinach) from the surrounding hills to this small market.

These *venditori* (vendors) are just some of the thousands of Italians who start their morning in the wee hours to bring the exceptional produce of fresh fruit, vegetables, fish, meat and cheese to the markets that are the lifeblood of the Italian kitchen. All over Italy, in small villages and large cities, under cover and in the open air, the morning comes alive at the local market. The produce is laid out with a simplicity and style that any *Vogue* stylist would envy: tomatoes are polished and stacked to form pyramids; succulent olives — black, green, marinated — glisten in their brine or are displayed in old-fashioned tins with Sophia Loren types painted on the sides; water is sprayed over live seafood in colourful blue and red trays, wetting the dark pavement; and soft *mozzarella*, aged *pecorino romano*, *parmigiano*, *burrata Pugliese* and *marzolino* are cut into enormous slabs and piled on top of each other. The atmosphere buzzes as the locals swap stories and recipes, and the aromas of basil, parsley and rosemary tint the air.

This morning I feel a tiny bit uncomfortable as Giovanna explains the subtle details of how to cook Tuscan *fagioli* (white beans), while a group of patient customers wait behind me. Giovanna's hands follow her words and dart around in the air as though she were dicing the garlic, pouring the beans from the steaming water into a bowl and squeezing the juice from an orange. Her eyebrows rise as she emphasises the importance of cooking the beans well but 'not so they fall apart'. '*Hai capito?*' (Do you understand?) she asks, not quite sure if I have all the subtleties ingrained in my memory. I glance at the *signora* (lady) next to me and apologise. She leans across, puts her hand on my arm and says, '*Non c'è fretta*' (There is no hurry). I return to the details of boiling, tossing and heating white beans in olive oil, safe in the knowledge that Giovanna will take the same amount of time and care with each of the customers behind me.

My celery, carrots and apples are lovingly placed in brown paper

bags and handed to me as though they were eggshells. Most mornings the
veggies come with a cooking tip — a special way of cleaning beetroots, or
blanching tomatoes so the skins come off easily or, as Giovanna offers today,
a much-loved recipe. We always finish with her breaking off a couple of small
bunches of herbs — today it's basil and parsley — that I insist on paying for
and she insists on giving to me before shooing me away with a warm light
in her eyes, murmuring, '*Vai, bella; domani, domani*' (Off you go, beautiful;
tomorrow, tomorrow).

I live in Florence but I have left my heart in markets all over Italy. If I close
my eyes I can still smell the coffee and hear the laughter as those spirited
napoletani unloaded their produce at one of my favourite Italian markets.
The sun had just broken over Vesuvius and the Bay of Naples. I asked a
Totò (Naples' most beloved comedian) look-alike where I could get a good
coffee. 'Carraturo,' he croaked, years of cigarettes echoing the words.
'*Cara, prova anche le sfogliatelle, sono buone lì*' (While you're there try the
sfogliatella, they're good there), he called after me as he lit another Marlboro
and resumed the business of lounging on a Vespa that was past its prime.
I found my way to the streets around Porta Nolana and entered Carraturo
as instructed; it seemed as if half the market had managed to squeeze
themselves into the bar. Rows and rows of heavenly freshly baked pastries
dusted with icing sugar sat neatly behind glass. I perched myself on one of
the stools near the bar, sipped the sweet black liquid that is *caffè* (coffee) in
Naples, indulged the *barista* (barman) who couldn't help but have a harmless
flirt and inhaled the aroma of sweet ricotta baking. By the time it came to
pay, *la signora* (the lady) at the cash register informed me that one of the guys

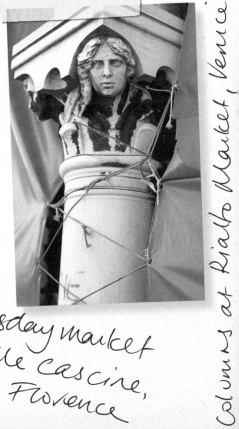

...celery, carrots and apples are lovingly placed in brown paper bags and handed to me as though they were eggshells.

Tuesday market alle cascine, Florence

Columns at Rialto Market, Venice

The boys selling contraband cigarettes, Naples

from the market had paid for mine on the way out. Welcome to Naples!

Naples' most famous market is a sprawling, open-air, sensual affair. Loud voices echo through the streets calling out the prices of *polpi* (octopus), the local specialty. Laughter and joviality float in the air, and water cools the live *cozze* (mussels), *vongole* (clams) and *scampi* (scampi) that jump and jostle in the brightly coloured trays. Rows and rows of the best seasonal vegetables and bread stacked up like bricks surround the base of a turreted tower. Small, simple cafes are squeezed in among the *bancerelle*, dispensing hot, strong black coffee that Naples and her *acqua* (water) have made famous. Vested waiters flit around the market carrying trays filled with espresso in shot glasses covered with little serviettes twisted in a special way to form a lid. Stalls of contraband cigarettes are dotted between the mozzarella, zucchini, flowers and sole. Vespas carrying two and three people weave in and out of the throng, dodging the shoppers laden with bags. Dark-haired lotharios sell everything imaginable. '*Asshhhpettt!*' (Wwwaaaiittt!) is heard as they dash out the back to get the item they have put away for their best customer.

By nine o'clock the market is in full swing. Women, men and children fill the streets; and the singsong of the fish vendors escalates. Naples' markets have transfixed travellers over the centuries with their bawdiness and *gioia di vivere* (joy of living). That fine spring morning I joined the ranks of the fallen.

You can tell a lot about an Italian city by its market. No two are the same. Bologna, at the same hour, is an elegant affair. Once an open-air market, the streets around Via Caprarie have been converted to chic little shops with open fronts, giving a stylish market feel. The Bolognese love their food and are proud of their tradition and reputation. *Le donne* (the women) here dress like *signore*: ermine fur coats in winter topped with little fur hats, Ferragamo slingbacks, kid gloves with cashmere lining and Hermès shopping

bags are seen among the glistening pyramid of strawberries, colourful capsicums and enormous parmesan wheels. Mortadella, salami and provolone cheese hang like giant bunches of grapes from the ceiling of shops such as Tamburini and Simoni. Elegant cafes line the streets around the markets, and white-jacketed waiters serve coffee to the Bolognese who call in on their way home. Conversations are peppered with the rich recipes that typify the Bolognese cuisine and the lavish way in which they enjoy life.

In Florence at the same hour, the famous Florentine accent that pronounces 'h' instead of 'c' fills the air as the *macellai* (butchers), *ortolani* (greengrocers) and *pescivendoli* (fishmongers) go about the business of setting up for the day, calling to each other through the corridors of Mercato Centrale. It's freezing; there is not a person in sight who isn't wearing a hat, scarf, gloves and heavy jacket. Everyone is huddled around Bar Piero with steaming glasses of *caffè latte*, wrapped together in that special camaraderie of a cold winter's morning. '*Come sei hhharina?*' (Aren't you cute?) echoes from somewhere near the *pescheria* (fishmonger's shop) as a beautiful girl passes by. Mercato di Sant'Ambrogio and Mercato Centrale in Florence might not be quite as elegant as the market in Bologna, but they are wonderful just the same. There is nothing like Tuscan pride in their produce and cuisine, and cold winter mornings aren't enough to deter me from being part of their special world, even if it's only for an hour or so. I go just to hear them pronounce *cocomero* — only in Tuscany does watermelon become a strange fruit known as *hohomero* and a cute girl becomes *harina* instead of *carina*.

The cheapest gondola ride you will ever take in Venice is from the Santa Sophia wharf to the morning market next to Venice's famous Ponte di Rialto. Standing up, balancing your way across the Grand Canal with faded *palazzi* (palaces) and emerald-green water as a backdrop has to be

Fish Market, Naples

christmas tree delivery

Naples

Naples

Naples

Naples

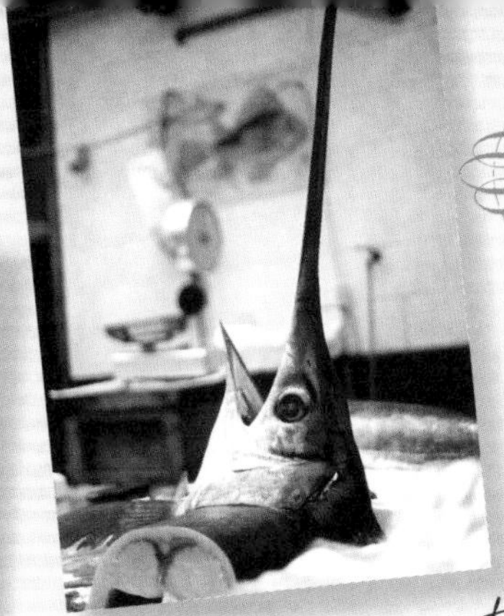

€uro

€ 0,84 KILO

Mercato centrale, Florence

Naples

the most beautiful way to arrive at a market. The Venetians make it look easy, and it's worth each of the 40 cents it costs. Bright red canvas, coloured flags, luminous white ice and rosy pink salmon can't match the colour of the Venetian *pescivendoli* as they call to each other, 'Ahhhooohhh' (Hey). The snow and driving rain don't touch the warm atmosphere the *venditori* create in their magical kingdom under the porticoes near the Ponte di Rialto. Boats, fish and beautiful women carved into the columns have watched over daily market scenes for more than 600 years.

In the summer of 2003 I begged Francesco to take me to the market in Bari, near his home town in southern Italy. It was August and I was secretly frightened that the market would be closed and I would miss my opportunity to see one of the south's most talked-about markets. We rose early and drove into the old city. Francesco's family was concerned because Bari has a tough reputation of being home to pickpockets and *motorino*-style bag snatchings. It is only recently that the centre has opened to tourists. The centre of Bari is picturesque: white stone houses opening on to white stone streets; every entrance is flanked by a colourful tabernacle of the Madonna or San Nicola (Saint Nicholas, the patron saint of Bari); kids play in the streets; and the smell of washing lingers in the air. An ancient building next to the port has long been home to the fish markets, and when we arrived it all looked a little quieter than I had imagined.

 Pesce (fish) and *frutti di mare* (seafood, or literally, 'fruit of the sea', such as *cozze, vongole* and *scampi*) are a fundamental part of the Mediterranean diet, so in southern Italy you can generally be guaranteed that there is a fantastic fish market. Our luck was in that steamy August

morning. A group of fishermen sat outside as they cleaned mussels and octopus, talking and laughing. I desperately wanted to take a photo of this roguish group. Water cascaded onto the pavement, the colour blue was everywhere — blue tubs, blue T-shirts and blue eyes — as though they had transported a little of the ocean and the sky back to the market with them. I politely asked if I could take a shot. '*A voglia te*,' (As many as you want) replied the oldest. '*Stai attenta, sono così brutti che romperanno il tuo obiettivo*,' (Be careful, though, they'll break your lens they are soooo ugly) he said, laughing and motioning towards his friends.

With that comment the rogue with eyes bluer than the sea grabbed a live octopus and said, '*Non c'è nessuno bello come me qui. Fai la foto bella*,' (There is no one more beautiful in this place than me. Take the photo, beautiful) his eyes reflecting the same light I see in Giovanna's eyes as she tucks the *prezzemolo* (parsley) into my bag in Santo Spirito. It's the same light that sparkles in the eye of Beppe the cheese seller at Sant'Ambrogio as he passes a fresh piece of *marzolino* across the counter. It's the laughter that lives in the eyes of Gennaro as he wraps the *scampi* in the newspaper cones each morning and offers *caffè* and *sfogliatella* (a crescent-shaped pastry filled with sweet ricotta and cinnamon) to every pretty woman that passes by. It's the light that says *amicizia* (friendship) as Dino presses a mandarin into my hand on an icy Venetian morning. When *il bello* grabbed the octopus and started to laugh, another small piece of my heart was left with another of those special Italians that live their life in the market.

blue tubs, blue T-shirts, blue eyes — Bari

Neptune from
Trevi Fountain -
Rome

the bar

Empty tables at Giuli Caffè, Florence

ISOLABE

VERMOUTH

The grey footpath glistens with rain, slick and shiny with the golden reflection of the street lamps. It's still early, around four in the afternoon, but it's almost dark. The bell tinkles softly as I push open the door to Pasquale's bar. It's full: the local *falegname* (carpenter) smoking at the bar, a *signora* (lady) with a fur coat and matching hat, Giorgio from the darkroom around the corner and Pasquale behind the *banco* (bar). The smell of freshly ground coffee and smoke mingle and rise to form a small halo-like cloud above them all. All sorts of different *caffè* (coffee) in different stages and *tazze* and *tazzine* (cups and little cups) sit along the *banco*. A half-drunk espresso sits in front of *la signora*, a *caffè lungo* (long black) for the *falegname* and a *caffè macchiato* for Giorgio. Voices are raised discussing world politics as cigarettes draw circles in the air and hands fly in time with the words.

The warmth beckons me in and Pasquale calls, 'Oooooohh, *bella*.' I listen to the conversation that is in full flight at the bar. It's the hour of *il salotto* (the lounge room), when the day is almost done and an Italian bar takes on a slower pace and conversations can last for hours. Pasquale leans across the bar and puts my two hands between his, warming them and greeting me at the same time. '*Allora bella mia, è abbastanza freddo per te?*' (So beautiful; is it cold enough for you?) My *caffè macchiato* arrives without me uttering a word. *Il falegname* is holding court, and I join in the spirited

conversation about the state of the world and revel in the sensation of an
Italian bar.

I can't quite remember how or why I first entered Pasquale's bar on Borgo
Pinti. I love the bar's simplicity and honesty away from the razzamatazz of
downtown Florence. A bar runs the full length of the cafe, and mirrors reflect
bottle after bottle of exotic Italian liqueurs: Sambuca, Strega, Punt-e Mes,
Martini Bianco and the local Tuscan favourite, Vinsanto. There are four small
tables with tablecloths that change from summer to winter and there is always
a copy of *La Nazione* and *La Repubblica* for customers to read. Obviously
the regulars don't come here for the décor — we come for Pasquale and his
brother, Antonio.

     No matter how far away from Australia I am, I always search out
places where I can feel at home; Pasquale's bar is one of those places for
me in Florence. It doesn't matter what time of day, what season or in what
mood I enter, when I hear the welcoming voice of Pasquale call '*Harlina*'
(Little Carla, with the 'c' becoming a Florentine 'h'), I immediately feel at
home. Pasquale is a historian, a social commentator, a *barista* (barman) and
a generous soul all wrapped together dispensing wonderful *caffè* in a place
I love. Leaning up against Pasquale's bar, sipping *caffè macchiato* I have
learned in which *vicolo* (alley) writer Vasco Pratolini lived, how the Arno
broke its banks in 1966 and nearly carried away Florence, and the words
to '*Firenze stanotte sei bella*' ('Florence, tonight you're beautiful'). I also
learned to speak Italian at this bar, Pasquale patiently coaxing another word
out of me, never laughing at my pronunciation and applauding me when I
finally got something right. Pasquale's bar is a club without membership, and

I adore entering to the hiss of the coffee machine and seeing the regulars who come to pass a part of their day with Pasquale.

My fascination with people such as Pasquale and the wonderful atmosphere they create behind the bar started almost the moment I arrived in Italy. When I discovered that most Italians take *colazione* (breakfast) at the bar, I couldn't trade in quickly enough cornflakes and cold milk for warm brioche filled with marmalade, chocolate, apple or sweet custard and the milky cappuccino that accompanies it.

I would slip in through the side door of Rivoire in Piazza della Signoria, letting the splendour of ornate chandeliers and the sweetness of chocolate, freshly baked pastries and ground coffee wash over me. Every day I would try a brioche with a different filling and always a cappuccino. The bar would fill and empty in the space of minutes, *signori* taking their *colazione* standing at the bar, coming and going on their way to work. Over warm brioche they would discuss their lives with the *barista*, telling him of plans for the summer, a newborn baby or *il nuovo amore* (the new love) in their life. The sounds of saucers being laid out on the marble bar, cups being lifted and gently rested back in their saucers and teaspoons touching porcelain would clink in the background. The espresso machine works overtime. Every detail is beautiful, including pear-shaped silver sugar shakers that make even sugaring your coffee glamorous. White-jacketed waiters open the door, always with a cheerful greeting, 'Buongiorno, bellina' and a smile.

Popi was right when she told me that the *camerieri* (waiters) and *baristi* (barmen) at Rivoire were *signori* (gentlemen). When I first came to Italy they would patiently make me a cappuccino after lunch without raising their eyebrows or telling me that in Italy you only drink coffee with milk in the morning. They explained that *vetro* (glass) didn't detract from the flavour of coffee, and serving a *caffè macchiato* in a *tazze* (big cup) not a *tazzine* (little cup) would make it cool far too quickly. They remembered my name, fussed over me when I entered, and pushed a small chocolate heart into my hand as I left. Breakfast at home, even in Italy, was no longer an option when worlds like Rivoire existed and beckoned me each morning.

Rivoire may have been my first love, but the thing I adore most about bars is that no matter how grand or simple they are — whether it's Rome, Naples, Turin, Venice, a tiny village in the hills of Tuscany or the flat countryside of Puglia — there is a strong chance that over your cappuccino or Martini Bianco you will have a random conversation with the person standing next to you, the *barista* pouring your drink or the *signori* who have stopped in for an *aperitivo*.

When my parents visited Italy in 2003, my father became as fascinated by Italian bars as I am. He loved the way in which Italians inhabit their bars, and he marvelled at their multi-function — it wasn't a cafe, it wasn't a pub, it wasn't a wine bar; it was a little of everything together. At three o'clock Mum could have a coffee, Dad could have a glass of red wine or an *amaro* and, when it was a hot summer's day, I could have my favourite gelato, *nocciola* (hazelnut), all together in the same place.

Dad was convinced he was at the centre of civilisation when on a hot summer's evening around seven o'clock we entered Rivoire, where the bar was set out for *l'aperitivo*, the time when Italians gravitate to the bar for *qualcosa da bere* (something to drink) and a snack to whet their appetite before dinner. Little plates of pasta, marinated olives, bubbling red sauces,

mini *panini* filled with the delicate flavour of truffles, prosciutto, pecorino, *patatine* (potato chips) and nuts all arrive unannounced, regardless of which bar and in which city you find yourself for that sweet hour before dinner. When Dad took his first sip of '98 Brunello, I could see in his eyes that passing his old age in a small apartment in Italy mightn't be a bad idea.

It's through the eyes and stories of *i baristi* such as Pasquale that I came to know an Italy that has already passed. When you could still swim in the Arno on a hot August day. When families sat around tables in the small *vicoli* (alleys) around Santa Croce, laughing and eating. When all the *contadini* (farmers) would gather together in Piazza del Duomo and wait to see whether the Easter *colombina* (dove) soared or fell, deciding the fate of their crops for the coming season. When the scents of *salsicce e fagioli* (sausages and beans) came alive as the workers in the hills of Tuscany broke for lunch on warm September mornings many years ago.

It's *i baristi* who told me in which church to find the Caravaggio near La Forcella in Naples, the best place to eat *polpette* (meatballs) in Venice, the way to Pizzeria Da Michele for the best pizza in Spaccanapoli, the words to 'Sapore di mare' ('The taste of the sea') and every nuance about their respective cities and history. They drew a smiling face on my cappuccino when tears rolled down my cheeks. They cheered me up by showing me a secret *cortile* (courtyard) hidden behind a fading Tuscan wall. They were the first to exit their bar and whistle down the street to their friend to take me to a small *piazza* housing a neon-lit Madonna I never would have discovered on my own. They directed me to the best stalls selling *granita* or a little *piazza* where an old lady makes orecchiette in the afternoon sunshine.

Pasquale

Paskowski
barmen,
Florence

cute
barmen,
Carraturo,
Naples.

Barmen
Gambrinus Caffe,
Naples

Making my cappuccino, Carraturo

Massimo @ Rivoire

Breakfast at home, even in Italy, was no longer an option when worlds like Rivoire existed and beckoned me each morning.

Thanks to *i baristi* all over Italy who have helped me, taught me and showed me an Italy I would never have found without them. To all of them (especially Pasquale), from the tip of Sicily to the border of Switzerland: thank you for your *caffè*, your *sfogliatelle*, *brioche* and *panini*, your laughter, stories and friendship. You made loving Italy easy.

l'estate

summer

Rocco ferries vs to Laurito

The last traces of *primavera* (spring) and its cool breeze are gone, and the warmth of the Tuscan sun has sent heavy jackets, long-sleeved shirts and trousers back to the wardrobe for another year. I am sitting on my bicycle savouring the sun on my back, waiting for the lights to change on Viale Europa. Out strides a beautiful woman with a low-cut top, long dark hair that swishes around her shoulders and long legs that finish in beautiful sandals. The sound of rubber tyres screeching to a halt and buses nearly piling into each other along the *viale* (avenue) are accompanied by motorists sitting on their horns in protest.

The drivers have taken their eyes off the road and allowed them to rest on the beautiful woman for a moment too long. I imagine the sounds of neck muscles snapping as men turn every which way to feast their eyes upon her. Like so many other girls who have had their first taste of summer, this woman has opted for something more revealing than a puffer jacket that is required to fight off the winter cold. The brunette passes, *ancheggiando* (hips swinging) in that special way that only Italians seem to move, loving the attention and the chaos her presence has created. She disappears along the footpath and the traffic seems to breathe a collective sigh of relief as they all go back to the business of ordered mayhem that the Italians call driving.

This near-incident will occur time and time again as summer comes

closer and clothing becomes skimpier. In the coming months, slowing down to admire a pair of beautiful legs in a short skirt, a slim ankle or a cleavage bursting out of a top will become a hindrance and a danger to Italian traffic.

Summer is the season that best reflects the exuberant nature of Italians. They dream of a long hot summer all through the freezing days and nights of winter. Summer holidays for Italians mean *il mare* (the seaside) and are always taken in *agosto* (August). Discussions about where they will go and what they will do for their holiday start trickling through bars in late May. Over a Campari in the afternoon they decide whether this year they will go somewhere they have never been or will return to *il solito posto* (the same place) they have gone every year for the past twenty years. They will probably opt for the latter. They will go with the same people and stay in the same house, meeting up with the same Italians who have also been going there for almost a lifetime.

The first summer I arrived in Italy I had no idea how an Italian city functioned in August. I imagined that, like in most cities around the world, everything would remain open and life would go on as usual. I was wrong. Italian cities become ghost towns as small red, green and yellow signs are attached to the *serranda* (shutter) of nearly every business. The signs read 'Siamo in ferie' (We are on holidays), with the dates printed below, and are regulation in Italy. That first summer I was stranded without any film when my local supplier took a month off. I arrived at my photo lab to find a note tacked to their door saying that they also wouldn't be back for a month. My favourite *panini* and wine bar, I Fratellini, pulled down their *serranda* one day and they too were gone for a month. The city emptied, leaving only the

Cossies on the line, Forte dei Marmi

Sunbaking on the rocks, Giovinazzo

Karen & Joe

Sun - lover
Philippa

fountain,
Villa Cimbrone,
Ravello

boats, Giovinazzo

tourists to the sweltering heat of Piazza della Signoria and the Ponte Vecchio.

One of the greatest benefits of living in Italy has been the number of eager visitors from home I have had each year. Fortunately, all my wonderful Australian friends love Italy as much as I do, and most of them have found their way to my door at least once in the past five years. The allure of an Italian summer holiday in the middle of an Australian winter is always irresistible. During my first summer in Italy, when the temperatures escalated and the population in Florence dwindled, I decided there was only one thing left to do: join the Italians *al mare* (at the seaside). I made two quick phone calls: one to my dear friend Karen in Australia and the other to my sun-loving Swiss friend Philippa (whom I met at Popi's table). Karen booked herself on the next available flight and Philippa jumped on the next train. After I secured the last spare room for the three of us at Maria Luisa, a small *pensione* in Positano on the Amalfi Coast, we were off to paradise.

The tiny village of Positano with its magical coloured houses clinging to the cliff was bursting with Italians. Most mornings we floated down the hill and caught a small wooden boat to Laurito, a nearby beach. The Italian beach experience was completely new to me. (My memories of going to the beach in Australia included dragging everything with me: towel, chair, umbrella and esky filled with cold drinks and sandwiches. If we were lucky we lasted a few hours under the sun's harsh rays before the wind picked up, caking sand to our bodies, sandwiches and beach bags as we headed home.)

Arriving at Laurito was like entering a 1950s Italian movie. Colourful striped *lettini* (beach beds) were neatly lined up. Everybody was on first-name terms. Italians love the sun and they love to sunbake. They oil their bodies and bake themselves for hours, turning their skin a deep mahogany.

positano = paradise

arriving at Sant'angelo, Ischia

Bikinis by Dolce & Gabbana, Blumarine and Versace are changed two and three times during the day, because *la bella figura* (looking good) is just as important on holiday as it is at home. *L'abbronzatura* (the tan) becomes the focal point of the summer and will be one of the most important topics for discussion when the Italians return to the city. The first time I asked for an umbrella at the beach the locals all glanced at each other with a knowing look — *è straniera* (she's a foreigner) — and returned to the business of tanning some more, not understanding why anyone would come all the way to the beach and not want the deepest possible tan.

At 1 p.m. precisely the *lettini* emptied and the entire population of the beach transferred to Da Adolfo, the small restaurant at the back of the beach. The restaurant was slightly elevated from the sand, allowing for a perfect view of the Mediterranean. The view was not interrupted by windows, doors or walls; the only structure in Da Adolfo was a simple iron roof that blocked the midday sun but not the soft breeze that floated in. Modern-day versions of Jackie O and Brigitte Bardot in capri pants and head scarves arrived in old wooden boats ferried from the millionaires' yachts anchored offshore.

'Would you like to try some cheese from Piedmont?' asked Marco, arriving with a plateful of cheese and salami and a bottle of red wine. Marco wasn't a waiter or even the owner; he was a devotee of Laurito, on holiday from Turin with his wife and daughter for the tenth year running. They had brought with them a little extra local product typical of the Piedmont region of northern Italy, and he was busily handing it around the tables. 'Where are you girls from?' he asked, and then, without waiting to hear the reply, 'How long are you staying in Positano?' 'Just a couple of days,' we replied in unison. 'We want to see the Amalfi Coast.' Marco smirked a little, raised his

eyebrows, clinked our glasses and, with a knowing look of someone who was shipwrecked here a long time ago, said, 'See you tomorrow.'

Our waiter, Alessandro, arrived in board shorts and bare feet and gave his recommendation for the day. 'Leave it to me,' he said. Like a genie, he got it right. On fresh lemon leaves from the hills of Positano arrived melted *mozzarella di bufala* (buffalo mozzarella) with the delicate infused flavour of lemons, and a ceramic jug of white wine flavoured with fresh peaches. This was followed by band fish — a local fish found in the Mediterranean — that had been caught mere hours before and grilled to perfection. As the afternoon passed, we lingered over lunch till four and then took our places back on the beach, forgetting about life, and spent the afternoon in and out of the emerald-green water.

Days rolled one into the other and the locals became our friends. One night the *ragazzi* (guys) from Laurito offered to show us the Amalfi Coast by night. Karen, Philippa, myself and seven *napoletani* (Neapolitans) piled into an old wooden boat and sang all the way to Amalfi, the moon lighting our way, the breeze lifting our hair and me feeling something close to love for this beautiful place. When it was time to head back to Florence and '*Pppppossssitttano*' was called for the last time, I was already nostalgic for the wonderful summer just passed. As the light broke up over the hill, turning the water silver, I inhaled the scent of lemons and salt, wanting to remember that smell forever. I too promised myself that I would return to this small piece of paradise next year.

L'estate is by far my favourite *stagione* (season). Not just because it heats up and I can swim in the divinely warm and calm waters of the Mediterranean

Procession of the Madonna, Positano

Chashy — Gisvinazzo

sleeping angel

or Tyrrhenian seas but because of the wonderful *gioia* (joy) that is generated in small villages throughout southern Italy. Traditionally, summer is the season of the *raccolto* (harvest), the time in which Italians harvest their crops and *festeggiare* (celebrate) a year of hard work. The local village *festa* (party) is the highlight of summer and the locals enjoy a week of festivities. *Piazze* (squares) fill with stalls overflowing with local produce, bands playing music and couples dancing, and the joy of summer comes alive.

Summer is also the season of *l'amore estivo* (summer love). Young couples can be seen smooching under lamplight or holding hands *passeggiando* (walking) along the beach. Summer is the biggest opportunity of the year to get to know someone who isn't from the local village, and the passion generated in summer has inspired hundreds of songs.

When the lovers wave goodbye to each other and head back to the cities or their village, *il rientro* (the return) becomes Italy's last memory of summer. Italians love to do things together; they love to do the shopping together, go to the theatre together and they love to return from their summer holidays together. They pack their bags and their car and attempt *il rientro* to Rome, Milan, Florence, Turin and Bologna. Television channels give live coverage of *il rientro*. Images of traffic banked up and snaking for miles are repeated time and time again. It doesn't matter which city, the traffic and *il rientro* are the same.

'*Quando sei rientrato?*' (When did you return?), '*Come era il rientro?*' (How was the return?) and '*Io sono rientrato . . .*' (I returned . . .) are the opening phrases to most conversations in bars for the next two months. The Italians explain how they came back, how many hours they sat in the traffic, where they went — every detail is examined. '*Che bella abbronzatura*' (What a great tan) becomes as familiar to my ears as '*Ciao bella*'. Women

and men alike admire each other's *abbronzatura* — the darker the tan the greater the compliments.

Being Australian and having lived in a city *sul mare* (on the water), I have always taken summer and the beach for granted. Australian summers last forever and the sun's warmth is like an old friend, never far away. Last year in Italy, winter was long. Snow sat on the mountains above Florence, breathing ice, killing the plants in the fields and sending the elegant Italians indoors to the refuge of a burning fire. I too was holed up in my apartment for a couple of months dying to get out. I started to dream of summer. Every time I opened the bathroom door and a blast of cold from the Arctic filled my apartment, I imagined tiptoeing down that small wooden plank to the beach at Laurito to warm emerald-green waters and brightly coloured wooden boats. I closed my eyes and inhaled the scent of salt air mixed with lemons, and watched a group of *napoletani* singing their hearts out under a silvery moon all the way to Amalfi. And I wished for an Italian summer without an end.

S. RITA DA CAS

the
Italians

Signora Cipriani at Palazzo Gerini,
Firenze

San Marco, Venice

I still marvel at the way Italians look at each other, openly staring, admiring and sizing each other up. It's only recently that I have stopped glancing in shop windows to check that everything is in its correct place. I would touch my hair, check that my breasts weren't bursting out of my shirt and that my fly wasn't undone. Why were they all looking at me? In Darlinghurst I could have walked the streets naked with barely an eyebrow being raised, but leaving the house here stops traffic. When I would pass two men mid conversation they would fumble over their words, losing their train of thought as though Cindy Crawford had just sailed by. I would look down at the footpath and hurry by, pretending not to see them as they smiled and uttered *complimenti* (compliments). I was confused by their reaction; passing from the invisible to the visible by simply boarding a plane in Sydney and arriving in Florence was difficult to digest in such a short amount of time.

In Florence, every morning as I exited my apartment building and went about my day, my fragile ego was resuscitated back to life. '*Che occhi belli*' (What beautiful eyes) greeted me at the bar, '*Bellezza in bicicletta*' (Beauty on the bike) as I crossed the Ponte Vecchio and '*Come sei bella oggi*' (How beautiful you are today) as I popped into my local store on my way home. Everybody was telling me I was beautiful, a phenomenon that had never happened on this scale in my life.

Eventually, my step had a spring in it. Instead of looking down as before, I would look men straight in the eye the way the Italian women did, and every now and then I would accept a coffee from a charming stranger who had politely offered it. Men rushed to my side to put my luggage on the overhead rack on the train; on a sultry summer's day they helped me over the *ponte* (bridge) in Venice; they pulled my chair out for me to sit down; and slowly they brought out the woman in me who had been hidden away for years.

A steady stream of *bei ragazzi* (handsome guys) found their way to my door and whisked me away on the back of their *motorini* (mopeds). Francesco, Marco and Salvo held the door open for me to enter a bar, insisted on seeing me to my front door when I wanted to go home and considered it a dent to their pride if I offered to pay my share of the bill. They recounted the path of Ulysses as though they had followed it themselves, and they knew the myth behind every Greek god, about most of whom I had only vaguely heard. Their conversations were peppered with words such as *carino* (cute) to describe a bar, or *bellino* (beautiful) to describe a film we had just seen, and it wasn't uncommon for them to rush over to a pram and coo over a baby, calling, '*Vieni, vieni*' (Come, come) to me. They thought rugby was a strange type of lettuce, preferred red wine to beer and stroked my hair as tears tumbled down my cheeks at the movies.

Italian men are like no others I had encountered before. All the rules I knew about dating and being with men were scrapped; they were obsolete in Italy. Italians love being together in big groups: old men and women, young couples and singles, sisters, brothers, aunts, uncles, friends and

children are always included and almost nothing is done alone. Italian men and women interact completely differently to those in Australia, and the longer I live here the more fascinating their dance of love has become to me.

One day while killing time at the railway station in Rome I was waiting in a bar when a girl walked in; a cloud of Acqua di Sicilia (a perfume reminiscent of oranges and lemons and summer in Sicily) followed her. She sat near me, taking off her checked jacket and balancing it on the tips of her shoulders. She wore a soft black woollen scarf doubled twice around her neck and a pair of black leather gloves, and she was carrying a designer handbag. As she moved to light her cigarette, men and lighters appeared from everywhere. She delicately balanced the cigarette between her fingers and slowly inhaled, her mouth caressing the cigarette. From underneath her lashes she glanced up and breathed *grazie* (thank you) to the man who had fallen over himself to light it. As she exhaled, her face and neck straightened like that of a ballerina ready to dance. The entire bar followed her every move, collectively pausing, exhaling and moving their heads with her as though they were all watching a game of tennis. The girl wasn't beautiful in a classic way, but her every movement was delicate and precise and created an allure of sexiness around her. The light seemed to go out when she finished her cigarette, put on her jacket and left the bar. Little scenes like this go on all day throughout Italy — lighting a cigarette, buying a train ticket or waiting in a bar is an opportunity to partake in the national sport of flirting.

Mr Patu
(Patu in Puglia)

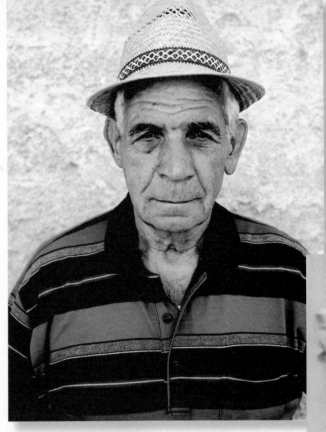

Ladies in Piazza della Repubblica

Silvia
in the foyer
of her office
(nice office)

Sarah in Palazzo Strozzi

ladies
matching
rome

My best friend in Italy, Silvia, is an Italian version of the 1970s model —
actress Marisa Berenson. Silvia was my first insight into the innate elegance
of Italian women. Two of the things that attracted me to Silvia when I first
met her in a Florentine restaurant when I was on holiday in 1998 were her
style and her gregarious nature. Perched in a corner chair with a colourful
modern fresco as a backdrop, she was the most stylish woman I had ever
laid eyes on. A white jersey dress from the seventies clung to her curves
and giant coloured beads cascaded down her cleavage. Silver diamante-
covered sandals decorated her feet. A cigarette enclosed in a mother of
pearl cigarette holder was perched permanently between her lips. Silvia's
two beautiful friends Marta and Luciana only added to the picture, all three
tanned and glowing. We just needed Jackie O and Truman Capote to walk
in and the flashback to an earlier, ultra-chic era would have been complete.
That night two gorgeous Italian waiters, Stefano and Ivan, insisted that *tutte
le belle ragazze* (all the beautiful girls) share a table, and thus began a night
of laughter and fun as we tried to communicate in the universal language of
hand signals.

When I returned to Italy to live and I had learned enough Italian to
pick up the phone and explain to Silvia who I was, I made the call that started
a wonderful friendship. Silvia became my fashion guru, my love adviser
and *la mia amica* (my friend). As a starting point to our friendship we had
one major thing in common — we were both diehard fashion victims. I had
arrived in designer heaven, and even though it was sweet torture for me to
pass the windows of Pucci, Miu Miu and Luisa Via Roma knowing I couldn't
just walk in and shop up, for us it was an instant bond.

Silvia showed me the Italian way. `*Tacchi, tacchi e solo tacchi,*` (heels,
heels and only heels) she would insist. Not only does Silvia walk in them,

Giant face, Cortile Campidoglio, Rome

gt art hand,
cortile
Campidoglio,
Rome

she glides, saunters and runs for trains in them. Silvia does everything with style: she ties her belt with just the right amount of *buon gusto* (good taste), and her scarf is folded and tucked into her jacket à la Grace Kelly. In winter Silvia trades slinky jersey for smart coats with fur around the hood, stilettos for the latest season's boots, and hands adorned with diamante rings for cashmere-lined gloves.

But her real secret, like that of all those stunningly groomed Italian women, is without a doubt her crowning glory: her hair. An Italian woman would never consider leaving the house with her hair wet or quickly pulled up into a ponytail. Her *parrucchière* (hairdresser) and a great-quality *phon* (hairdryer) are an Italian woman's best friends, and the results are scenes that resemble a giant hair commercial where long glossy hair cascades in curls or hangs perfectly straight and is held in place with designer sunglasses.

Like most Italian women, Silvia is very feminine and has an inner confidence about her looks and body that I have rarely seen in Australia. It's all in the way she moves, the way she holds her head and tilts her chin to meet a man's gaze — you can almost hear her purring.

When I moved to Italy, kissing my American Express card goodbye gave me no other choice than to embrace a new style of fashion, which (thank God) I have always loved: boho chic. Silvia dragged me to all her favourite second-hand markets, where it seemed that glamorous countesses had left the contents of their wardrobes for the likes of me. Glorious cashmere jumpers were piled up like coloured lollies, tailored jackets hung neatly in rows and every now and then a Pucci scarf went undetected.

The fashionista in me lived on in a completely new way in Italy. Here, old men sport berets and Persol sunglasses, leopard skin abounds on the shoulders of smart *signore* (ladies) in leather pants, and hats of every kind

Here, old men sport berets
and Persol sunglasses,
leopard skin abounds on
the shoulders of smart
signore in leather pants,
and hats of every kind
along with scarves
and gloves are de rigueur.
Italians of all ages
are fashion mad.

ladies chatting—
at the Excelsior Hotel, Florence

along with scarves and gloves are *de rigueur*. Italians of all ages are fashion mad, and I soon felt right at home.

Appearances in Italy can be very deceiving. One of the many times Trenitalia was running late and all the passengers were stuck together not knowing what was happening, the guy next to me started a conversation, introducing himself as Mario. I presumed he was a bank executive from Milan having a weekend off. Mario, whose skin was beautifully hydrated as though he had a facial once a month, wore the latest pair of Prada shoes, a cashmere throw jumper in the perfect shade of caramel loosely tied around his neck and a pair of hip Diesel jeans. I found out during our *guasto* (breakdown) that Mario was in fact a *gommista* (tyre repairer) from a small village in Calabria. I have since given up trying to discern what a person does or where they come from by what they are wearing. It's impossible.

I won't even pretend to have come close to really understanding Italians. How could I ever understand that on a suffocating 35-degree day, barely a puff of wind coming in a train window could possibly cause a *blocco* (chill) to the neck of a *signora* sitting five rows away? Or that as my Italian friend seats himself at my table complaining of a bad back, he insists it was caused by the fan that his wife used the previous night to combat the freak 45-degree weather? Try telling an Australian who never changed their wet swimming costume in their life that it could be dangerous to your health and cause a *blocco* in your stomach and ruin your digestion for the day. How could you not love a race that goes on holidays en masse in Greece with a *fazzoletto* (handkerchief) around their neck, protecting them from *il vento* (the wind) and yet another *blocco*?

heels, heels and any heels.

Blocchi aside, I find Italians funny, flirtatious, elegant and sometimes highly frustrating. They make the most divine shoes in the world, have the most gorgeous churches and art, and even the garbage collectors manage to look like supermodels. They cook like kings and make the most heavenly coffee, but my favourite quality is their innate kindness towards others.

As the years have passed I have regularly witnessed the Italians' kindness and generosity towards others less fortunate than themselves. When a small boy enters a restaurant on a cold winter's night with a giant bunch of roses to sell, the staff don't send him scurrying away; they let him go about his job, sometimes buying the whole lot for their female clients, making his night's work short and a lot of women happy. When a blind man walks along the footpath with his white cane, bravely dodging bicycles and roadworks, someone will link their arm through his and guide him across the road at the traffic lights to make sure no harm comes his way. At 2 p.m. when Casalinga (a busy *trattoria*) is in full swing and the line of patiently waiting clients extends out the door, a customer in a beautiful suit slips a 20 euro note to Beppe, a familiar *barbone* (homeless person), so Beppe won't go hungry for lunch.

Many wonderful worlds have been opened to me because of the Italians' ease and generosity towards others. Entering a barber shop on a Saturday morning in Naples not only got me an offer of a *caffè* but an invitation to the wedding an hour later of the guy being shaved in the barber's chair. Asking to take a photo of a family eating lunch on the footpath on a hot afternoon in Puglia turned into a three-hour lunch sampling the home cooking of yet another generous soul. When Popi and I took the wrong train to the wedding of Eric — our Ivy League friend from when I first arrived at Popi's house — and were stranded at the border of Austria, it was

nothing for an Italian *signore* (gentleman) waiting for his daughter to drive us 90 kilometres out of his way to get us there on time. And on a cold winter's night when the wind whips rain onto my face and I thank God I have a home to go to, the sight of a *barbone* exiting one of Florence's best restaurants with a giant *focaccia* stuffed with *buone cose* (good things) reinforces to me who *gli Italiani* really are.

Trevi Fountain—Rome

happy eating

buon appetito

1 o'clock, Casalinga,
Florence

At 1 p.m. precisely, like a national school bell ringing, the metallic sound of *serrande* (shutters) closing and shops shutting buzzes through the streets. It's the sound of *pranzo* (lunch) in Italy. Buying a light bulb, an onion, an ink refill for your computer or a new bra in most Italian cities is impossible between 1 p.m. and 3 p.m. when workers head home or to a local *trattoria* to pass two hours savouring their lunch. Big brands such as Fendi, Prada and Gucci slip a silver key in the door, pull in the mat and usher their customers to the door, wishing them *buon appetito*. At this time of the day in Italy, what's important is what to eat, where to eat and with whom to eat.

Francesco and I have a little circuit of traditional *trattorie* where we go for lunch when I'm not making something at home or eating with friends. Today is one of those icy winter days when a strong wind blows off the river Arno and I crave the warmth of somewhere familiar. We make our way through Nuvoli, the tiny bar packed with Florentines drinking red wine, to the *osteria* (eating place) downstairs. Rosano's father commands the tiny bar upstairs, and when he spots us he clenches our hands and kisses both cheeks. '*Che bella coppia*,' (What a beautiful couple) he announces to the bar, squeezing our hands with delight. We make our way down the rickety stairs into the warm atmosphere of the *cantina* (cellar), where dusty bottles of Chianti red wine line the walls. Faded black-and-white photographs of an ancient

Italy are stuck to the exposed stone and solid wooden tables are already full as we encounter the noise and colour of the lunchtime crowd. Nuvoli has no written menu, just the voice of Rosano and his daily specials. We take a seat next to a businessman who is already devouring *ribollita* and *pasta al forno* (baked pasta), and the smiling face of Rosano appears as he ducks his head, navigating the stairs. *Pane* (bread), *vino* (wine) and *acqua* (water) arrive without our asking, and, like father, like son, he too announces to the assembled crowd, '*Che bella coppia*.'

Food glorious food surrounds us, and it is impossible to choose as Rosano rattles off the menu: *ravioli con crema di tartufo* (ravioli with a cream truffle sauce), *rigatoni con salsa piccante* (rigatoni with a hot tomato sauce), *spaghetti con ragù* (spaghetti Bolognese), *pappa al pomodoro* (a rich Tuscan soup made of tomatoes and bread) and *crostini toscani* (traditional Tuscan starters). He flies up and down the stairs with plate after plate of steaming pasta, always smiling and joking as the customers call to him from all corners of the *cantina*. When the *primi* (first) and *secondi* (second) dishes have been devoured and the bread has cleaned the last traces of *sugo* from our plates, Rosano runs off the list of *dolci* (desserts). Francesco and I decline the list of *tiramasù*, *pannacotta* and *castagnaccio*, but he brings a plate of *castagnaccio* (a thin cake made from chestnut flour) just the same, insisting '*Ti fa bene*' (It's good for you).

Lunching at Nuvoli — or, for that matter, at Il Contadino, Anita or Casalinga — is almost like eating at home or with an Italian family. Checked tablecloths or brown paper cover the tables. Simple glasses and carafes fill and empty as the *primi*, *secondi* and *contorni* (side dishes of vegetables) arrive. *Il padrone* (the owner) never has a menu; his wife, sons and daughters keep the place running smoothly. The beauty is its simplicity. Lunch isn't

about fine dining or eating out; it's the Italians' way of spending their *pranzo* together in a place with the right food and the right company, at the right price.

When I first arrived at Popi's table I thought her way of living was unique: three courses every night, the table laid with simple cutlery, crockery and always a tablecloth. I have since learned that the celebration of food happens in almost every Italian home, every day and night. It was never any trouble for Popi to set an extra plate if someone arrived unexpectedly. She would almost clap her hands with delight at the thought of another person at her table, and she would always emphasise the importance of being and eating together. In even the simplest of homes, the table will always be set, a *primo* and a *secondo* will be served, and you are expected to take your time and enjoy the food that has been prepared with love.

Preparation, cooking, eating and discussing the subtlest details of food are as fundamental as love to daily Italian life. Recipes or cooking tips are offered in almost every imaginable situation: the taxi queue at the station, the old man selling vegetables from the back of his little Ape (tiny truck) in Piazza Santo Spirito, the food store in Via del Croce or the cute guy in the bike shop. Italians were born in the kitchen and this is a nation of chefs who produce five-star meals at home.

Love is in every gesture. In the tomatoes that have been lovingly laid out in the June sun to dry. In the olives hand-picked by the family to produce olive oil that will grace their table for the coming year and enhance everything from *insalata* (salad) to *fave* (broad beans) and *cicoria* (chicory) with its glorious taste. Love is in the homemade *panini* (rolls) stuffed with mortadella tucked into my hand for my train trip back to Florence. It's in

lunch @ casalinga

waiter takes me order 'Da Rocco'

Angiolino

scampi on the grill, Positano

Baking brioche, Naples

Mum, Spaghetti in the kitchen of Tre Sorelle, Positano

the staff eating lunch at Lauríto

the speed and generosity with which a stranger will invite you to share something special they have made and encourage you to *mangiare* (eat) as much as you want. In Italy food is music to the soul, and the soul is fed and nurtured with love at least three times a day. It's what makes Italians so uniquely content with life.

I don't know how many times I have stood in the *piazza* at San Pierino with a group of my Italian friends discussing what we will make for dinner together. '*Salmone con crema di capperi*,' (Salmon with a light cream sauce flavoured with capers) suggests Attilio, then Luigi pipes in that he feels like *linguine con cozze* (linguine with mussels), and they are all off reciting the ingredients by heart. Twenty minutes may have passed before Attilio remembers that his mother has sent homemade *culurgionis* (a pasta similar to ravioli only the centre is filled with pecorino, mashed potato, butter and mint — yuuuummm) and a big piece of pecorino from Sardinia. After thirty minutes of debating what the menu will be, we decide to make a fresh tomato *sugo* (sauce) with a hint of *salvia* (sage) to go with Attilio's mum's *culurgionis*. In true Italian style, all five of us head to the local store and the fruit and vegetable cart in the *piazza* to buy the ingredients. My friends would never consider a quick takeaway meal because it's easier. Italians feel cheated if they are made to eat on the run or in a hurry.

Another night, when friends were coming for dinner at 8 p.m. and at 7 p.m. I still hadn't done the shopping or bothered looking in a recipe book, I knew as I raced down the stairs to the store that the shopkeeper would know the exact ingredients I would require for *pasta e fagioli* (pasta with beans), *pollo alla cacciatora* (chicken in a red wine sauce) and *tiramisù*. Some days I go from shop to shop, buying things I have never tried before, and it's enough just to ask, '*Che cosa si fa con questo?*' (What do you make with

panini and
the world
Cup –
Happy days!

water melon = summer in Sicily

this?) and the owner is off and running with just the right amounts to make *cipolline in agrodolce* (sweet-and-sour onions) or some other delicacy. Other customers chime in occasionally when they have a special tip they prefer, and the whole shop comes to a halt to debate that particular recipe. No-one ever complains about the wait; they all seem to enjoy the moment — after all, it is their favourite topic.

Another thing I adore about eating in Italy is the seasonal produce and regional specialities. Even though to foreigners Italy is Italy, to Italians Italy is still broken up into twenty regions. Ask someone, '*Di dove sei?*' (Where are you from?) and they will probably answer, '*Sono Calabrese*' or '*Veneziano*' or '*Fiorentino*' or '*Sardo*', rarely '*Italiano*'. Garibaldi may have united Italy over 100 years ago, but as far as the Italians are concerned, firstly they are '*Pugliese*' or '*Siciliano*' and secondly '*Italiano*'. The wonderful thing about this is the diversity it brings to every region's culture, architecture and cuisine.

Regional specialities make travelling anywhere in Italy a highlight. Even though these days I can track down *taralli* (crunchy savoury biscuits) in Florence, there's nothing like eating them fresh with the flavour of aniseed at Francesco's mother's house in Puglia. Some bars in Florence make *sfogliatella*, but savouring the sweet ricotta and flaky pastry with Vesuvius looming over you and Vespas tearing by in Naples seems to heighten the rich sweetness. And we all know that tortellini is made all over the world these days, but as I buy it from Atti & Sons in Bologna, freshly made that morning and wrapped in paper and string, I am convinced that nothing has ever tasted better. You will never convince a Florentine that a big slice of pizza with mozzarella, garlic and fresh

tomatoes is better than those little *panini con la trippa* (tripe rolls) they sell from little caravans around the city.

Regional food links me to some of my favourite travel memories of Italy. The first time my Venetian friend Marco dragged me into a small bar near the markets at Rialto on a cold windy night for a *polpetta* (small rissole) and a glass of red wine, I thought I had died and gone to heaven. As the rain poured outside I couldn't stop at one *polpetta*; I devoured cheese, meat and every flavour the owner's wife had made. My Pugliese friend Tommaso makes the most heavenly *linguine con cozze* (linguine with mussels) for us in his tiny kitchen in Florence. We love sitting around his table soaking up the garlic, parsley and white wine sauce with Tuscan bread. But nothing compares to eating *linguine con cozze* sitting on a director's chair with pebbles under your feet with the soft wind blowing in from the Mediterranean and a dozen wooden boats bobbing on the horizon at Da Adolfo's in Positano.

Another thing I adore is the giant brown paper packages tied up with string that arrive at my friends' homes on a regular basis from all over Italy. Mothers who are worried about what their sons are eating pack giant slabs of homemade pecorino, olive oil, pasta from *Nonna* and the essential red wine for every meal into boxes and faithfully mail them off with *la posta* (the post). Tommaso, Attilio, Francesco and Luigi become the lucky recipients of homemade *culurgionis*, orecchiette, hand-pressed olive oil and a crumbly slice made from apples and honey — a gourmet's heaven that any five-star restaurant would be proud of, but to them it's just home cooking from *Mamma*.

sunshine and orecchiette—Bari

Zucchini flowers, Mercato Santo Spirito

Atti's
Spaghett

famiglia e gli amici

family and friends

three generations, Spaccanapoli, Naples

Anr'c

I grew up in a family full of life. Four children in five years must have seemed like a good idea to my mum, and, as though four noisy kids weren't enough, there was always a menagerie of cats, dogs, chickens, rabbits and the odd tortoise. My mother had the spirit of an Italian, even if she didn't have the corresponding culinary skills, God love her. It was mashed potatoes, sausages, veal cutlets, roast dinners and the cookbook of the 1950s Australian housewife for us. The door was always open and the light afternoon breeze would bring with it an unending stream of neighbours and friends requiring a cup of tea, some advice or just a chat. The table was a ritual in our family. Every night it was set for the six of us plus an extra place for anyone who might drop in.

Mum and Dad weren't unlike Italian parents in many ways. Dad was always in the garden tending his tomatoes, sweet peas and poppies, and Mum remained at home to look after her brood and do everything in her power to ensure we grew up with love and care. Each weekend we would pile into the Valiant and head to a local river, dam or beach where we would meet other families and the kids would run wild, jump in puddles, swim and climb trees as though the world were ours.

It has been with the passage of time that I have realised that my parents gave me something money can't buy: their can-do spirit. They told me that there was nothing in life I couldn't do, and I ended up believing in it as a modern-day affirmation. I know that when I left Australia in 2000, it was difficult for them to wave me off at the airport, not really knowing where I was going or when I'd be back. As I passed through the steel departure doors two things remained etched in my heart and mind: the warmth of their embrace and those magic words, 'Whatever it is you want in life, love, you know you can do it.'

The first night I came to Popi's house in Florence and took a seat at her table, it felt so familiar. It was something I had done so many times in my childhood. After years as an adult eating alone, on the run and always in a hurry, taking a seat at Popi's table was like stepping back in time. Wonderful memories of nights locked together in the warmth of my family came flooding back.

Living at Popi's house was my baptism into an Italian family. Popi's sister, Maria, lived downstairs and called up from the balcony below whenever she needed Popi or *una cipolla* (an onion) to finish the evening meal. Their parents had lived their whole lives in that house, ensuring that Popi and Maria would always be looked after. Easter, Christmas and Sundays were big occasions for the family and their friends to get together. The table was always the gathering place — at Easter it would be laden with *uova benedette* (eggs blessed) and lamb roasted with *rosmarino* (rosemary); at Christmas there was *il cappone lesso* (roast rooster); and on Sundays were three courses that went on forever.

At around 1 p.m. most Sundays the doorbell would ring — Popi's family arriving from all corners of Florence. Popi's daughter, Monica, and her man, Ettore, from the hills of Tuscany; Maria and Renzo from downstairs; and Popi's crazy cousin Silvio would scream to a halt outside on his Vespa —

La famiglia e gli amici
Family and friends
167

these and all of their corresponding children were welcomed with open arms. 'The golden girls' would always arrive first: Popi's lifelong friends Maria Pia, Giovanna, Silvana and Carlina, each one perfectly coiffured and glamorous.

Sometimes I would sit quietly amid the smoke and listen to the conversation, marvelling at their honesty towards each other. Every now and then I would cringe at comments that were just a little too direct for my Anglo-Saxon upbringing, although I loved the theatrics of it all. In dramatic Italian style, they raised their voices, waved their hands in the air, feigned mock indignation and then forgot all about it the next day — after all, they are family.

As I made friends with Italians from different parts of Italy, I also got to know their families and their wonderful ways. My friend Silvia regularly invited me to her mother's home in a small village on the outskirts of Tuscany, where the extended Matteoli family would unite each Sunday. When the sun lowered over the hills of San Miniato, the remnants of four courses became sweet memories. As the *grappa* and *caffè* were poured, cars would arrive bursting with friends of the family weighed down with gifts of cold bottles of *Prosecco* and mouth-watering pastries tied up with string. I knew as I looked out to the houses dotted among the olive trees that all over Italy around tables were families gathered to share Sundays together just like the one I was experiencing.

I soon realised that it didn't matter if you came from different regions or socioeconomic situations; the common denominator in Italy is the strength of an Italian family. Like an impenetrable force the extended Italian family works together, nurtures and helps each other in every way. Parents,

Wedding Naples

gorgeous Michele—

Popo's family friend

La famiglia e gli amici
Family and friends
171

brothers, sisters, aunts, uncles and cousins make up the family business, tend the family's *orto* (vegetable garden) and take their *passeggiata* (evening stroll) together in the centre of their village dressed in their latest finery. And when the time comes for one of the *figli* (children) to be baptised, take their first communion or marry, the Italian family turns out in all its force.

Italians are loved and adored from the minute the little blue or pink bow announcing their birth goes up on apartment doors, windows and shops. Children are sacred in Italy. All you have to do is enter a restaurant with a *squadra* (team) of noisy kids and you will see the waiters dropping plates of steaming pasta and momentarily forgetting their customers to bound over to hug, hold and fuss over the *bambini*.

Most Italian children, no matter where they live in Italy, return home to spend the summer with their family. So it has become a natural part of my summer to make the trip from Florence to Francesco's family's home in Terlizzi. Francesco's family have made me feel a part of them, and when August arrives I love heading south to the delights of sundried tomatoes on the *terrazzo* (terrace) and the warmth of a very special Italian family. In the summer of 2004 while visiting Francesco's family, it finally hit me why Italians grow up to be such an affectionate race. Sitting among four generations of Cataldi women in Francesco's grandmother's lounge room, I witnessed them hugging, caressing and telling two gorgeous baby girls how beautiful they were for hours on end. At the beach I saw a father singing softly to his baby daughter for three hours holding her, never once letting her tiny feet touch the ground. And at the end of the summer when our train sped north, I watched a small boy of six being cradled to sleep in his father's arms, safe in the love of the embrace and the admiring smiles of the passengers around him. Touch and affection never ceases in an Italian family, no matter how old you grow.

Picking tomatoes,
Puglia

mother and
daughter —
Quartieri
Spagnol,
Naples.

Friends, Trapani
Sicily

'Backstage',
first communion
Lotzorai
Sardinia

La famiglia e gli amici
Family and friends
173

tabernacle, Naples

Aunt &
nephew,
Pugna

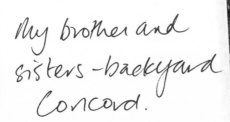

My brother and
sisters - backyard
Concord.

Nuns, Florence

La famiglia e gli amici
Family and friends
176

For me, living in Italy has stripped back life to expose what truly counts.
Time and time again it has revealed to me that life isn't about climbing the
corporate ladder, working late nights and leaving the office when the city
is dark. It isn't about driving the latest car and having smart dinner parties
where only even numbers are acceptable. And it certainly isn't about eating
takeaway Thai food alone night after night. Life is about people and the
emotions we share with them. It's about the real *ricchezza* (wealth) in
life — family and friends.

     As I go about my day in Italy, the Italian family is visible everywhere.
When I finish a roll of film, it is developed by two brothers, Gianni and
Danieli. When I slip into Pasquale's bar and he makes me a *caffè macchiato*
before I can utter the words, it's his brother, Antonio, who hands me my
brioche. When I enter the *ortolano* (greengrocer) on the corner of Via Maggio
to stock up on zucchinis, it's the father-and-sons team of Guiseppe, Luigi
and Domenico who vie for my attention. As I slip another succulent slab of
mozzarella di bufala (buffalo mozzarella) into my bag, it's Signora Rossi and
her son, Fabio, who ask after *il mio amore* (my love). And when, at the end
of the day, I pull my bike up at I Fratellini to savour a glass of red wine,
it's Michele and Armando, the brothers at I Fratellini (little brothers) who
indulge me with yet another Italian tale.

     You enter the lives of Italian shopkeepers once and they politely assist
you. You enter twice and somehow you leave knowing all their names. You
enter for the third time and you instantly make up part of their extended
family. So many times I have returned to Florence tired and exhausted
from a trip away, wondering what the hell I am doing in this place. As the
taxi weaves its way through the narrow dark streets, however, my tiredness
and despondency slowly evaporate as I pass the fountain of Buontalenti on

kids playing in the vicoli at night, Naples

tabernacle, Naple

La famiglia e gli amici
Family and friends
179

the corner of Via Maggio, Caffè degli Artigiani in Piazza della Passera and Piazza Santo Spirito and I think of the people who will be there tomorrow with their wide smiles and open arms. They make up part of my family in Florence.

Francesco has told me many different stories of his family and friends. How when he was young he spent most afternoons at his *nonna*'s house with the scent of *taralli* baking while she talked and answered the many questions that sprang from his curious mind. How his *zii* (aunts and uncles), who lived upstairs and around the corner, left their doors open for all the cousins, aunts and uncles to come and go as they pleased. When his mother called to him, ' *Vai dalla zia per piacere a prendermi l'olio?* ' (Can you please get some olive oil from your aunt?), it was just a matter of running up ten stairs to get it — and sometimes eating dinner twice when the aromas of her kitchen sidetracked him from his mission. How he, his brother and their cousins all go out together on Saturday nights like a bunch of old friends, not like more distant relatives.

My sister recently sent me a letter that moved me to tears. She told me all the things she loved and missed about me. How she loved me just popping in for a cup of tea and a chat and sitting in the backyard in the January sunshine while the kids played in the pool. On a trip home in 2004 Francesco and I had spent almost every day in and out of her house, taking the kids to the zoo and the beach and making them laugh until they cried. Sometimes it would hurt too much to think about leaving them again, so when the tears welled up in my eyes I would look away, pretending something had caught my attention.

I console myself with the idea that maybe one day we will all live near each other like Italians. We will have a plot of land that in summer

Neapolitans gathered
in the market to
watch the 2002
World Cup!
(Italy didn't win)

La famiglia e gli amici
Family and friends
181

will be loaded with ripe red tomatoes, bright orange melons, rocket, lettuce and enough olives to produce olive oil for my family. Donna, my wonderful big sister, and her family will live upstairs, and downstairs will be my little sister, Jan, with the noise and chaos of her house that I so love. And my brother, Stewart, will live across the road, always ready to help me when something breaks (hearts included) as he has done so many times in the past. And my parents will be close enough to live the life we lived when we were young, a life that I am sure as every day passes my mother misses more and more. As the years have passed I have learned to live without many Australian things, but I still haven't mastered living without my family and friends.

charlie and morena
christmas 2004
sydney.

la lavanderia

the laundrette

slippers in the sun — Naples

At home in Florence, my shoulders ache as I round the corner into Via de Serragli and head for my local *lavanderia* (laundrette). Two bags of washing are gathering weight and I happily empty them into the machine and rid myself of the *peso* (weight) for an hour. I thought my laundrette days were over, having moved into the world of 'grown-ups' a long time ago. I was the proud owner of a Fisher & Paykel washing machine that almost made me coffee at the same time as it did the washing. My clothes dryer was in constant use drying those last-minute things in my crisis-management style of running my personal life.

Now every Sunday morning while Florence grinds to a halt, I head down my steep stone staircase and across Piazza Santo Spirito in the direction of my *lavanderia*. The laundrette has been one of the many grounding experiences that have accompanied my change of lifestyle and living in Italy. Italians aren't appliance-mad. Machines that I have always taken for granted, such as fans, airconditioners, dishwashers, washing machines and dryers, are almost foreign objects to most Italians. I don't have one friend, or know of one person who has their home airconditioned or uses a clothes dryer.

Instead, washing is strung like proud banners from windows and balconies, or, as in Naples, across even the main streets to catch the sun's

rays. Vespas and old ladies dressed in black pass underneath while soccer boots, children's teddy bears, old ladies' underpants, sheets, jeans, tops, bras, slippers and every household item that can be washed fly high above for the world to see.

Even when I lived with Popi and the house was full with up to eight people, the washing was strung out most mornings from the second-floor windows and pulled in each afternoon, still warm from the sun. In the depths of winter the *stendino* (clothes rack) would come out and the clothes would be spread over it and dried by the heat of the house. Occasionally a *perizoma* (G-string) or sock would be lost to Popi's sister's balcony below, but the thought of buying a clothes dryer was never entertained.

Now that I live in my own apartment, I often look out into my *cortile* (courtyard) at my neighbours' 'personals' that are on display. The girl across the way delicately pegs her red bra and G-string for all to see. A big pair of white cotton undies that belongs to the old lady upstairs swings with the occasional puff of wind. The guy next door's long blue socks are so long they look like they must finish under his armpits.

I had a notion that outdoor clothes drying secretly related to looking good. Italians buy high-quality clothing in small quantities and they look after it. Francesco takes care with everything — the way he dresses, the simple way he put his possessions back in their place after he has used them and the way he eats his food. I couldn't understand when most times I wore half my lunch down the front of my shirt why not even a breadcrumb landed on his jumper. I discovered that it was all in the way he ate: slowly, never slouching in his chair, his back straight and his mouth perfectly positioned above his plate, small bites accompanied by a firm wipe across his mouth with a *tovagliolo* (napkin). Francesco always took the time to sit down, never

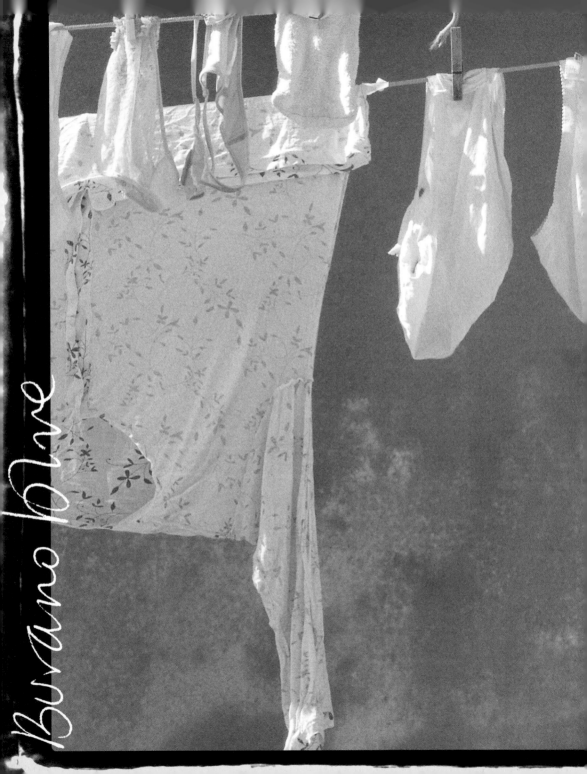

Burano Blue

AVE MARIA

618

ate in a hurry or on the run, and often would turn to me, saying, '*Piano, piano*, Carla' (Slowly, slowly, Carla), trying to break my lifetime habit of doing more than one thing at a time.

I started to ask every woman I met whether she had a clothes dryer: Renzo's wife at the store where I go every day, the lady on the bike next to me at the gym, the woman who sells newspapers at the station, friends of all ages. More than once they responded with, '*Che cosa?*' (What?) as though I had asked them if they wanted to go to the moon. It didn't matter how many women I asked, I couldn't find one who had a dryer tucked in the back corner of her apartment, villa or house. '*Che faccio io con un asciugatrice quando ho tutto questo spazio e sole?*' (What would I do with a dryer when I have all this space and sun?) was one of the responses as they motioned towards tiny balconies and lines strung from window to window. '*Non hai visto come i vestiti degli stranieri sono pieni di grinze?*' (Haven't you seen how crushed foreigners' clothes are?) was another. I asked Francesco's mother and aunts why they didn't have a dryer. I could imagine them rolling their eyes to yet another of my silly questions. '*Secondo te, io compro una macchina per rovinare i vestiti?*' (Why would I buy a machine to ruin my clothes?)

I am a convert and now drag my washed, wet clothes home from *la lavanderia* to put on my *stendino*. By the end of the day they are perfectly dry and still hold the scent of the washing powder. But above all, I love the flashes of my childhood days that come and go as I pull the sheets back every night and fall asleep with the scent of freshly washed sheets caressing my nose.

An advantage of outdoor clothes drying is the wonderful scent that fills the air in Italian towns. I believe that every Italian city has an aroma, and one of my favourite things about Naples is its *profumo* (perfume). The first time I explored the *vicoli* (alleys) of Spaccanapoli I was transfixed by

the strong scent of Dixan, one of Italy's best-selling washing powders. I didn't need to look skywards to check that washing was strung from every available balcony and window; the perfumed air confirmed everything.

Another of the small joys I have found in going to the laundrette has been the ritual of going to my laundrette bar on the corner of Via de Serragli and Via Sant'Agostino. It could be any bar in Italy. A couple of tables for those who really need to sit down; fluoro light overhead; sugar, chips and ashtrays line the *banco*. I come here on Sundays while my clothes are doing their thing at the laundrette. Today, the bar is filled with people, including an old man in a tweed jacket with a driving cap perched on his head, smoking and drinking a beer; and a young couple of German tourists sipping coffee and eating brioche.

I call this my 'wonder bar', primarily because it's here amid the smoke and clatter of teaspoons that I contemplate people and places, the past and the future. It was here in mid 2001 that I decided that, instead of hauling around heavy camera equipment as an assistant for another photographer, I would bite the bullet and try to make it as a freelance photographer. When the last few euros were jingling in my pocket, the romantic notion of being a 'starving artist' became a harsh reality and having my card returned at the automatic teller machine with a polite 'contact your bank' a regular occurrence.

The idea of buying a pair of the latest season's kitten heels was the farthest thing from my mind; it was more a question of whether I could feed myself or pay the rent. For the first time in my life I tasted poverty, and I felt the shame of looking my landlord in the eye and explaining why I was a few hundred euros short on the rent. I developed a new respect for all the money I had so flippantly wasted in the past and the freedom that money brings.

But each time I thought my guardian angel didn't exist, and living as a photographer in Italy wasn't an option, the phone would ring. It was always

CORTE DEL FONTEGO

5412A

Campo Santa Margherita, Venice

Cesarina full of life at Popi's window

washing drying, Burano, Venice

Scorted wrile - Bari

at a crucial moment, such as when a magazine called from London, asking
me if I wanted to go to Tuscany to shoot a story. Of course I did! I would
have gone anywhere; the only question for me was, when? That day, in the
hurry to get home I nearly mangled all my clothing as I extracted it from
the washing machine and then rushed home, skipping and singing and
hugging wet laundry to my heart.

Each Sunday that I arrived at my wonder bar was a small victory —
I had made it through another week. Living in Italy has made me feel like
Cinderella who finally got to go to the ball and landed smack-bang in the
middle of life. The excitement of packing my bags to go and photograph
everything from satanic cults in northern Italy to *Carnevale* in Venice for
Marie Claire, of shooting minimalist hotels and glamorous parties at Palazzi
Pucci for *Harper's Bazaar* and jetting to Spain for *Qantas Magazine* made
living on a shoestring worthwhile.

The simple act of returning to do my washing at *la lavanderia* at
nearly forty years of age has evoked many thoughts. Having the time to do
a simple task such as cleaning my own apartment, washing my own clothes
or arranging jonquils in empty Campari bottles for my table are small things
that to me are a great luxury. Even when I had more money, I could never
'buy' enough time to do the simplest of things for myself. Looking after
myself is a wonderfully nurturing feeling that doesn't come with my house
being cleaned by a stranger, or my clothes arriving washed and delivered in
green plastic bags. There is something incredibly wonderful about having
enough time in my life, even if it's just to do my laundry.

Grandma
Springs
to mind
x

the Madonna

la madonna

The madonna in Easter procession,
Trapani, Sicily

At the end of August 2002, overwhelmed by the stifling heat of the summer sun as Florence's *piazze* filled with large tour groups, I decided to head south to breathe some fresh air. Every Florentine I know had warned me about the dangers of Naples; so many times, in fact, that it sounded just the place for me. Naples is, I was told, unlike any other Italian city. The idea that mayhem reigned, rules were ignored and a rich, raw life still existed, appealed to the adventurer in me. My friends promised me I would be robbed, followed and carried away by marauding bands of gun-toting *napoletani* (Neapolitans). They didn't know that most mornings when I raced out the door in Darlinghurst to work I would step over someone asleep on my doorstep and then politely nod to the pimps and pros manning each corner.

In the heart of Spaccanapoli I found a *pensione* (boarding house) run by Zia Carmela, Zia Rosa and four dogs that seemed to have more say than the *zie*. In the streets below was the Italy my wildest dreams could not have served up; the Italy from all those Fellini films crammed full of action and chaos. Children played soccer up against a faded church wall, *motorini* (mopeds) flew by with families going about their day, the voices of the fish vendors echoed through the streets and every possible stall lined the *vicoli* (alleys) selling every imaginable item. I hadn't walked 10 metres when I was

transfixed like one of those locked-gaze moments in a Mills & Boon love affair. It was like love at first sight. I was gone.

At the front of every house was a fluorescent tabernacle containing the face of Italy's most beautiful woman smiling back at me. Every corner I turned she was there surrounded by faded photos of lost loved ones, bunches of roses or lilies and a *lampadina* (small light bulb) to illuminate her face. At the bar she glowed out from between the bottles of *limonata* (lemonade) and cans of tomatoes. While old men played cards in the little rooms tucked in the side streets, she was there, life-sized, watching over them. Stars illuminated her head and flashed intermittently in shop windows. She hung above my bed in my *pensione* and was tucked in between the fruit and vegetables at the morning market. When I sank my teeth into pizza she was there hanging above the wood-fired oven with brightly coloured jewels crowning her head and the baby she held lovingly in her arms. She sat neatly in the visor of the taxi that dropped me at the *pensione*. When the fishermen arrived back first thing in the morning and displayed their wares at the market she was there looking down on them.

When I returned to the two mad *zie* the first night and sat down, I could hardly put my feet back on the ground, they were hurting so much from the Madonna frenzy that had kept me searching *strada* (street) after *strada* for more. The *zie* looked at me as if I were crazy when I asked who she was. '*È la Madonna!*' they responded in unison. '*Chi?*' (Who?) I asked, confused.

In the small kitchen, amid the heavenly scent of *maccheroni con ragù* (maccheroni with a meat sauce), Zia Carmela and Zia Rosa commenced my Italian religious education. I think they loved having a student sponge who soaked up every word they said, and they got a great kick out of me returning home every night enthusing at the beautiful new images of her that I had found

that day, as they patiently explained as much as they could. I loved the concept
of the beautiful tabernacles dotted all around the city with photos of loved ones
who had passed away, a fresh flower and a small lamp to illuminate their faces
and the hearts of those who missed their presence.

Twenty-five euros in Naples bought me the single room in which, if
I didn't roll over carefully in bed, I would end up on the floor. My room was
perfectly positioned between the bathroom and the toilet, which both seemed
to be in continuous use, but the warmth of the *napoletani* and the elaborate
Madonnas easily won over the tour groups in Florence's Piazza della Signoria.

So much for being robbed — it was the opposite. Every time I asked
to take a photograph, the *napoletani* insisted on giving me something to show
I was welcome. By midday on the first day I had consumed six coffees; my
pockets were overflowing with oranges and apples; I was the proud owner
of my first statue of Padre Pio, Italy's most recently anointed and most loved
saint; and I had received numerous offers to lunch from ladies I chatted
with in the street.

My first visit to Naples was to be a three-day stay but stretched into
a week, filled with afternoons spent listening to Zia Carmela singing Dean
Martin songs and mothers calling out to their children to come in for lunch
while I pounded the footpath in search of *la Madonna*.

I am the most unlikely person to have fallen in love with Italy's religious
iconic figure. My religious upbringing came to a swift halt on a warm
summer's morning in a small wooden church in the Australian countryside
when my younger brother was delivered a clout over the head with the Bible
from our local Sunday school minister to encourage him to 'calm down'.

Jesus, Terlizzi

Church door, Puglia

From that day we were released from hymns, polished shoes and starched clothing to the delights of Sundays in the country running through long grass, eating rosy-red watermelon and playing with our dog, Jedda. Mum maintained thereafter that religion could be practised anywhere, even at the kitchen sink: 'You don't need to be in a church full of people for God to know you're here.' Hence I had hardly set foot inside a church since I was five. Those intricate stories of the Bible that every Italian seemed to know by heart had been swapped for a killer tennis forehand and wonderful memories of Sundays with my family.

In Italy it was different — the Madonna and her beauty gave me a reason to put my head inside every church I could, and there is now hardly an oversized church door in Florence that I haven't pushed open at some time. When I go to *la lavanderia* (the laundrette) to do my washing and have twenty-five minutes for the cycle to finish, I love sneaking into the back row of Santo Spirito to gaze at the incredible light that filters through the high windows and illuminates her angelic face.

It started like a game to find as many different representations of her as I could, and it became a wonderful discovery of ingenuity, art, beauty and devotion. I stopped glancing ahead as I went about my day. Instead I cast my eyes upwards to the subdued Florentine Madonnas that sit high on the street corners. In Rome I hardly saw a footpath because it was impossible to take my eyes off the ochre *palazzi* in which she was ornately framed by stone angels. When we went to pick olives in Terlizzi she sat in the middle of the ancient groves watching over us, and when I took a short cut under a cool arch in Bari she was there watching over me like a guardian angel.

I quickly discovered that religion was part of everyday Italian life in many ways. Not only was *la Madonna* staring back at me wherever I went,

padre pio, Naples

Madonna, Erice, Sicily

the Pope gave his opinion on everything and was held in higher esteem than the prime minister. In the weeks prior to Easter a notice is tacked up on every *portone* (front door) to advise residents when they will be visited by a local priest to have their house *benedetta* (blessed). The priest arrives with *acqua santa* (holy water) and sprinkles it around the four corners of the house, blessing it and its occupants with peace and fortune for the coming year.

Most of Italy's public holidays are held in honour of a saint. Every city, town and village worships a patron saint or the Madonna as its protector. The saints and the Madonna are represented in varying forms, from elaborate paintings to life-size statues or ornate boxes containing their relics (just the saints of course!). Each town has a legend explaining how their saint or the Madonna came to be their protector. The *Madonna di Sovereto* (the protector of Terlizzi) was discovered when a *pecora* (sheep) got a hoof stuck in a crack in the ground. After the shepherd freed the sheep he noticed a divine light beneath the crack in the ground that led him to an ancient painting of the Madonna in the cave below. Others arrived on boats from far away. The bones of San Nicola (better known to the world as Saint Nicholas, or Father Christmas), patron saint of Bari, were stolen from Turkey and transported to Italy at the beginning of the first millennium. In Florence we celebrate 24 June for San Giovanni (St John the Baptist), our patron saint. The city closes down and the day culminates with fireworks to rival New Years Eve. One day my friend Rocco called to invite me down to southern Italy for his *onomastico*, something that in my limited Italian I had deduced wasn't his birthday, nor the day he was christened, nor an engagement celebration.

particularly mothers. La Madonna gave me a new respect for the women of the world who have borne, cared for, loved, raised and lost their children.

ladies walk for 24 hours,
following La Madonna
Trapani
Sicily.

After repeating '*Che cosa?*' (What?) for the fourth time I decided to simply respond, '*Sì, sì, verrò*' (Yes, yes, I will come), and then rushed off to check the word in my dictionary. The dictionary didn't explain it in enough detail — 'name day' — for my liking, so I went to Pasquale, my authority on everything. He laughed at me when I told him I was travelling to the south of Italy for someone's *onomastico* without knowing what it was. '*È il giorno del suo santo*' (It's his Saint's day), Pasquale explained, grabbing the calendar and flipping to the month of August and to the day of Rocco's *onomastico* — there in print was '*San Rocco*', the day Italy had dedicated to this saint.

I was very excited about the prospect of going to my first *onomastico*, wondering what awaited me. Sixteen friends, a wooden boat and the Amalfi Coast were the setting. Rocco's phone rang constantly with *auguri* (best wishes) from aunts, uncles and friends who were calling as though he had won the lottery or fathered a baby. When smaller boats passed us and their occupants recognised Rocco they too called *auguri* across the water. It was a party like any other party, except we were brought together in the honour of San Rocco, the protector of surgeons, pharmacists and prisoners, to name just a few.

I too have my own day, on 4 November for San Carlo, who is the protector of the clergy, teachers and 'makers of starch'. But I have 'adopted' Santa Rita as my preferred saint because she is the protector of women.

Once or sometimes twice a year, a statue of the patron saint is taken from the local church, carried on the shoulders of men in an elaborate religious procession through the town. This procession is the culmination of the village festival, which is usually held in honour of the patron saint. The village lights up like a birthday cake, and the main *piazze* fill with music, dancing and eager locals waiting for the procession. Incense floats on the air, deep voices echoing prayer pave the way and a strange stillness descends

when the procession arrives. Perfectly choreographed hands fly in time forming a cross as they pass. Old men in one fluid movement remove their hats and bow their heads.

Slowly all my friends got to know about my Madonna obsession and would offer titbits and advice to help me on my quest. I flew to Sicily to see *i misteri* (ancient carved wooden statues depicting twenty scenes of the Passion of Christ) and *la Madonna* in Italy's biggest religious procession at Easter. I was overcome with joy when Francesco took me to the centre of Bari to discover that among the beautiful white stone streets were 120 brightly coloured tabernacles to the Madonna, all decorated with little skirts of fabric. While all my friends were drinking *aperitivo* and watching the sun set over the Amalfi Coast I was following her along the beach behind priests scattering rose petals in her wake. A small sigh would escape my lips when I would enter a dark church where I had never been before to discover her in yet another form.

The more I saw her, the more I felt connected to women, particularly mothers. *La Madonna* gave me a new respect for the women of the world who have borne, cared for, loved, raised and lost their children. It's impossible not to be touched by the emotions portrayed by the Madonna. The eternal sadness of centuries of mothers is etched in the bow of her head, the agony on her face, in the silver ornamental sword through her heart and the lost child in her arms. And it made me think about my mother, who raised, cared for, loved and selflessly let me go.

Bologna

VIA
VOLTO SANTO

La

the Vespa

Vespa

Gioia, Naples

Side-saddle
Naples

It's five o'clock on a clear summer's morning, and the sun is rising over the horizon of the Amalfi Coast, turning the blue water to gold. It's cool enough to pull my jacket a little higher around my neck and move closer to the warmth of Francesco's body. I can't help singing as loudly as I can Blondie's 'I want that man' above the roar of Francesco's 1970s baby blue Vespa. My hair whips my face as we navigate the hair-raising bends and the sheer cliffs that fall to emerald-green water below. Lyrics from different songs flit into my mind, but they seem to pale into insignificance as the sun rises over the hill creating magic before my eyes. I inhale the scent of Francesco's neck (salt water and lemons, crisp morning air scented with trees) and I thank God I am living this moment. If Blondie hasn't found heaven yet, I know where she should look. Heaven is hanging on to someone you love on a baby blue Vespa at dawn, inhaling paradise as it flashes before your eyes in a myriad of colours on the Amalfi Coast with nature and the sound of a Vespa in the background.

In *Roman Holiday* it's difficult to discern which bewitched Audrey more — Gregory Peck or *la Vespa*. Sophia Loren rode through the tiny cobblestone streets of Naples, giving a two-wheeled motorbike more sex appeal than ever before. Anita Ekberg and Marcello Mastroianni were chased and photographed constantly by Vespa-packing paparazzi in *La Dolce Vita*. Millions of Italians, plus the odd Australian, have had an enduring love

Naples

affair with one of the most beautiful design objects of the twentieth century. If it was good enough for Audrey, Gregory, Sophia and Marcello, it's surely good enough for me.

There's a certain sound that comes with riding a Vespa that distinguishes it from the rest of the *motorini* (mopeds) hurtling around Italy. It's the sound it makes as the gears change down; it's a deep, musical sound that doesn't have that baby-crying 'wahhhhh-wahhhhh' sound that comes from the rest of the pack. And there is nothing like the sensation of attaching yourself to the back of a gorgeous Italian and flying through the streets on a Vespa — it's enough to make me want to rush out and buy capri pants, a silk Hermès headscarf (if I could only afford it), to-die-for sandals and black cat's-eye sunglasses.

Ochre walls, men smoking cigars, baroque fountains, locals drinking coffee and people on bikes all blur together from the seat of a Vespa. It's easy to understand how Audrey, Gregory, Sophia and Marcello fell in love with its sexy curves and little spare tyre on the back, and how effortlessly it became the symbol of Italy and freedom to thousands of young Italians who could finally afford a 'set of wheels'.

Every time a classic Vespa passes I can't help but stop and admire. It doesn't matter if it's crossing Ponte Santa Trìnita in the depths of winter or ferrying a family around Naples or the *lungomare* (sea front) of Bari, there is a unique beauty and magic in the Vespa's form that I find enchanting. I am intrigued by the people who ride them and I love the fact they haven't opted for one of the souped-up plastic scooters — that form doesn't do anything for the imagination and doesn't require a gear change. Let's face it: Audrey and Sophia would never have considered riding side-saddle on one of those.

No other part of Italy has embraced and retained their love of the original
'50 special' Vespa like southern Italy. In Naples, Sicily and parts of Rome it's
the only model you see on the road, in varying states, from mint condition to
held-together-with-rolls-of-Scotch-tape. Naples is a city that literally lives on a
Vespa; children grow up standing between the legs of their parents as they go to
buy pizza, visit an aunt or make their way to school. In Australia kids grow up by
the sea and learn to ride a surfboard before they can walk, and the Vespa is the
equivalent for kids in Naples. Neapolitan children ride a Vespa with an ease and
fluidity that comes with a lifetime of practice, surfing the mountainous streets
in and out of traffic as naturally as if they were launching themselves off the
crest of a wave. Neapolitans are so reluctant to part with a loved original that it is
often held together to the dying moment with everything from string, steel cord,
Maradona stickers and their favourite, Scotch tape.

The Vespa is more than just a vehicle to transport one around *centro*
(the centre of town); it's a way of life for many Italians who use it as a means to
deliver hot fragrant pizza, long planks of wood to building sites, new season's
plants and the entire family. The Vespa has lots of secondary uses when it's not
hurtling down cobblestone streets with mini-Marcellos on board. It becomes
the equivalent of an outdoor lounge chair on which dark-haired lotharios
recline in a nonchalant way that only Italians can pull off. The side mirrors
are perfect to check that the gel is still holding their 'do' in place or there is
no spinach stuck in their teeth before they roar off to pick up their *ragazza*
(girlfriend). Impromptu card games break out on seats, couples in the dark of
night make out and when two Vespas are parked together the outdoor *salotto*
(lounge room) comes alive, becoming part of the street furniture.

Italians from all walks of life take the Vespa option instead of the car.
Not just because it looks good, but because traffic is a huge problem in Italy.

a little girl in Naples

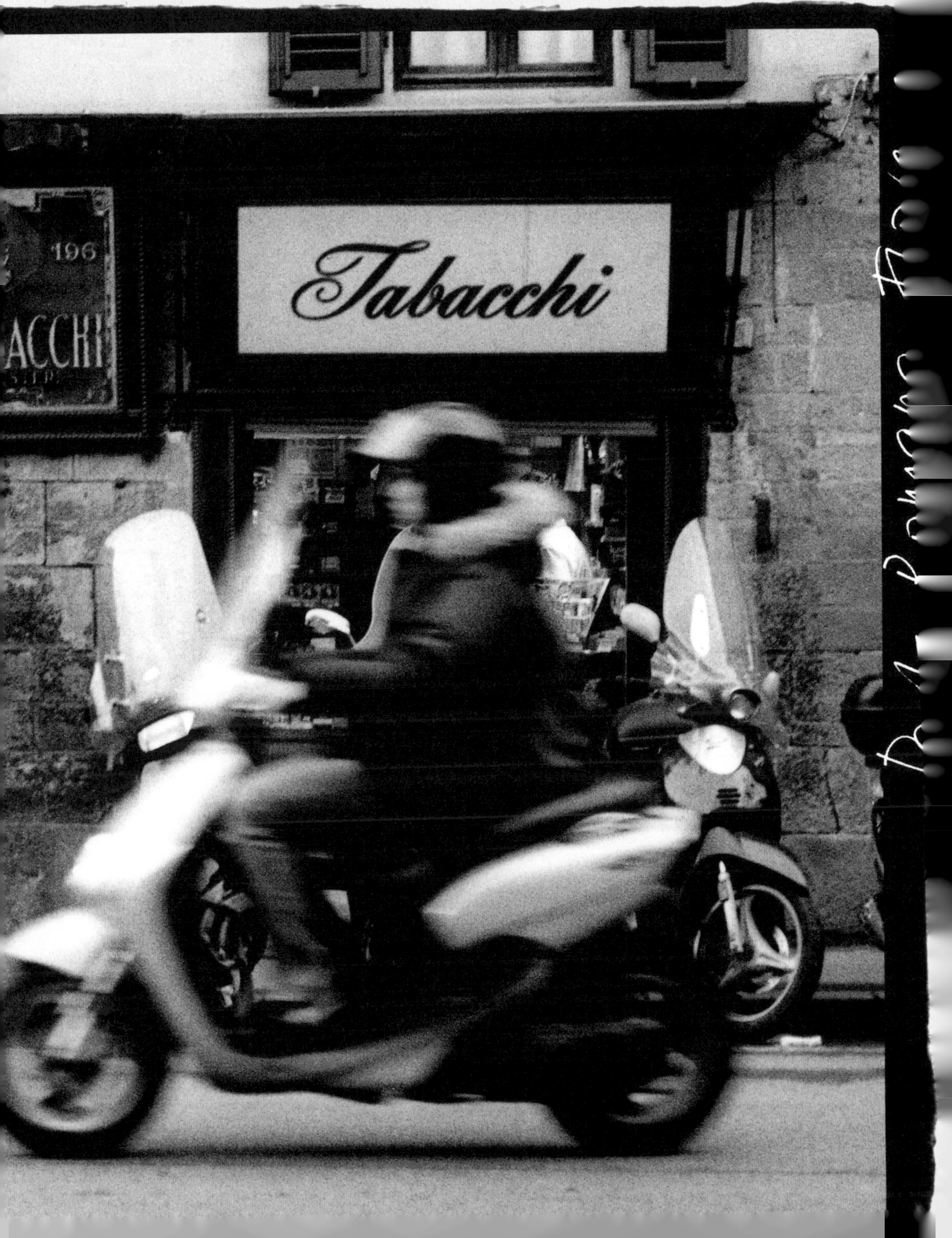
196
Tabacchi

Narrow roads that were built for horses and carts mean that traffic jams occur on a regular basis in all cities. Finding a parking spot can be a good enough reason not to own a car, hence the popularity of the two-wheeled *motorini*. Coal-eyed women with blue-black hair, outlined lips and tight pants fly pass with a mobile phone attached to one ear, leaving Italian men gaping in their wake. Middle-aged *signori* (gentlemen) in head-to-toe Armani carrying leather briefcases roar off at the lights in the morning like Valentino Rossi as they head to the office. The world's coolest grandfathers rest their grandchildren between their arms as they take the kids to school, and in summer, women in short skirts with bronzed legs literally stop traffic as they pull up at the lights.

When I am eighty years old and think back to all the beautiful moments in my life, I will remember the following 'Vespa moments' with more than a good dose of fondness. Sitting in Piazza Santa Croce with a group of my friends, five Vespas and a *fiasco* (straw-wrapped bottle) of Chianti wine when the rain set in and we were treated to the sight of my 'proper' English girlfriend riding back to her hotel with a giant umbrella covering two bodies, with just the wheels of an ancient Vespa visible . . . Doing laps of the Colosseum lit up at midnight thinking I would pass out from the beauty of it all . . . Squealing with joy the first time I rode away from Popi's house with Francesco, her yelling something down the street about helmuts and being careful . . . Screaming with sheer delight, fear and excitement as my mad friend Gennaro doubled me through the streets of Naples, dodging old ladies selling octopus, fruit and vegetables; to this day I can't remember even as a child on my first roller-coaster ride feeling so overwhelmed.

ponte santa trinita
Florence

Naples

which colour
would
you like?

kids, Naples

Lorenzo +
Pino,
Florence

And when the time comes for me to exit this world I will do it contentedly, knowing I lived one of those Blondie must-do moments, hugging the waist of a tall, dark, handsome tiger-eyed Italian, loving life on the back of a 1970s baby blue Vespa with one of the most beautiful coastlines and a piece of heaven before my eyes.

[left margin, handwritten, rotated:] ...dark of night make out and when two Vespas are parked together the outdoor salotto (lounge room) comes alive, becoming part of the street furniture.

Amalfi Coast

the journey

il viaggio

Venice

girl rides through Piazza della Repubblica in the rain – Florence

I feel like I have been travelling all my life. I took my first plane trip without my parents when I was four years old, and from that day onwards the love of travelling has been infused in my blood. The first weekend I was in Florence I went to the train station with a small bag, looked up at the destinations board and randomly selected somewhere I had never been before. I chose Urbino, checked the map to make sure I would make it that night, and set off on my first of many Italian adventures. At every opportunity I have returned to the station and looked up at the *partenze* (departures) with the same degree of excitement as the first time, loving the sensation that going to unknown places brings. The beauty and diversity of Italy and its *paesini* (small towns) intoxicated me from the beginning, and its charm has not worn off.

I have grown accustomed to travelling by train in Italy, and to the train stations with their elegant air of yesteryear, the queues that snake to the *biglietteria* (ticket office) and the occasional passenger who loses their head over a late train or a last-minute *sciopero* (strike). '*Lo sciopero*' along with '*Come si mangia?*' (What's the food like?) were two of the most important phrases I needed to learn in a hurry to equip myself in the early days. I learned like the Italians to plan my random weekends around the striking schedule to avoid spending more time than I had bargained for on a deserted platform in a remote part of Umbria or Le Marche.

I love watching the train fill and the scenes that play out on the platform: anticipation, elation, sadness, excitement, adventure and love in all its forms. It's there for all to see in the sharing of a cigarette as passengers board the train and in the eyes of a young girl as she guides an old lady to her seat. A polystyrene box filled with succulent *mozzarelle* that passes from a mother to her son as he boards the train from Bari to Milan, tears of anguish filling her eyes as the train pulls out from the station. A small voice that fills the carriage with excitement calling, '*Mamma, Mamma*' at the sight of a smiling woman jogging along the platform with tears of joy streaming down her face. Lovers of all ages dotted along the platform kissing with a tenderness of those who are saying goodbye, waiting for the station master's whistle to blow before making the dash for the closing doors. Mobile phones that ring all over the *carrozza* (carriage), bringing messages from *mamme* (mothers), *ragazze* (girlfriends) and *amici* (friends). '*Hai mangiato?*' (Have you eaten?) is always the most popular question, closely followed by '*Quando arrivi?*' (When do you arrive?)

I love the way an old couple unwrap their *panini* (rolls) and neatly lay them out for lunch with the preciseness of those who have done it a million times before. The raising of heads when the aroma of a strong salami wafts five rows forward and all the passengers crane their neck to see where it's coming from. Or a nun who has fallen asleep and snores softly while a red-haired woman next to her paints her nails red and feeds doggie biscuits to her poodle. And there is nothing like the camaraderie that naturally develops between passengers when the *capotreno* (train driver) announces we have just hit a goat and our train will be delayed for over an hour. Welcome to Italy.

Washing down the Orient Express, Venice

ticket office, florence

Sfogliatelle

florence

Bass buying
a ticket -
Bologna

Saying goodbye -
Florence

My first plane
trip with my
big sister.
(I'm on the right!)

Train travel offers moving pictures of seasons changing before your eyes, brown fields that a month ago were covered in snow but now burst with bright red poppies announcing spring. Ancient aqueducts scattered through green fields welcome us to Rome, and the first glimpse of the Adriatic glitters and seduces as we head south for the summer holidays. Train travel in Italy is a journey in the true sense of the word and one in which I partake willingly. One warm June afternoon as I carefully balanced twelve warm *sfogliatelle* on my knee from Naples to Florence, the rhythmic motion of the train and the sun streaming in the window transported me back to that fine Friday afternoon in Sydney when I knew I had no choice but to change my life. Deciding to leave my life was one thing, but knowing what I wanted was another.

At that point, there were very few things of which I was actually sure. What was clear to me was what I didn't want, but I had no idea what it was in life that I did want. I was willing to give up everything to find out what it was. When I waved goodbye to my friends and family and set off on my travels, I had no idea where I was going, how long I would be away and where it all would lead me.

Time and time again, people told me how brave I was to 'throw it all in'. I could imagine the confused look that must have crossed my face as they repeatedly uttered the word 'brave'. It had nothing to do with bravery. In fact, it was the opposite. A mixture of fear, frustration and anger was what pushed me to go. Fear that I would be trapped in a life that wasn't what I wanted; frustration that I would never find someone to love; and anger that it was all passing me by.

There was only one promise I made to myself as I packed the last remnants of my life into boxes and chose the things that would fit into two suitcases: I was going to spend the second part of my life doing something

I loved, something about which I was passionate.

Once I had made the decision to leave I was filled with the
exhilaration that change brings. Changing everything — how I had previously
lived, the language I spoke, the breakfast I ate, the time I got up, the people
I met on a daily basis — was for me the adventure I had craved. Like a puff
of oxygen that ignites a dying fire, I was reborn. Aromas were more pungent,
noises louder, colours brighter and feelings that I forgot existed came
flooding back like long-lost friends. My life became an emotional journey
and I an eager passenger, wherever it was going to take me, good or bad.

Though there were many good times, there were also times when
I thought I wasn't going to make it, that I just couldn't pull it off and that this
time I had really bitten off more than I could chew. There were days when
my stomach was filled with fear and tears of frustration would well in my
eyes, overflowing like a river down my face and on to my shirt. The idea of a
regular income became just a distant memory and was swapped for a roller-
coaster ride to survival.

But, every time I thought my dream of walking in the footsteps of
Annie Leibovitz and Ellen von Unwerth was about to be extinguished, a sign
would come, saving me from disaster and propelling me on. I truly believe
that someone was watching over me and didn't want me to give in. Time after
time, like small miracles from nowhere, the phone would ring. Photographing
fashion had never entered my mind, but when an Italian fashion magazine
called one day (a long time after my first job, for *Marie Claire*), it seemed
too good to be true, and I had no reason not to try. Overcome with nervous
excitement and gut-wrenching fear at the thought of failing in front of
models, make-up artists and an editor with more *gusto* (good taste) than
I had ever seen, I launched in with unbridled enthusiasm and did my first

kiss goodbye — Milan

Snow Florence from Piazzale, Michelangelo.

shoot for *Collezioni*. The editor clapped her hands together with delight when she saw my shots and hugged me as tears cascaded down my cheeks, overwhelmed by her reaction. I took hours to get home that day, riding my bike around in circles, lost in the joy of the moment, not believing that it was happening to me.

Moments such as this slowly became more frequent. By the summer of 2004 I had called Italy home for the best part of four years. I was regularly crisscrossing Italy for numerous Australian and international magazines and finding myself living one adventure after another thanks to my camera. The roller-coaster ride had moved into a new phase (fewer ATMs telling me to contact my bank). One of those beautiful summer afternoons in June of the same year, as I tucked a big, round mozzarella into my bag, adding it to the tomatoes, olives, parmesan, mushrooms and roses that sat in my bicycle basket, it struck me that all the good bits of life that were missing had finally arrived, better than I could have hoped. As I pedalled home the wrong way up Via Maggio, the wind lifting my hair off my face, I started to sing at the top of my voice, tears of joy rolling down my cheeks. The night before I had photographed one of Europe's most fabulous actresses and in two days I was going to Spain to shoot Flamenco dancers and matadors. The editor of *Collezioni* had just clapped her hands yet again over the last series of work I had done. Renzo, the owner of my local store, had insisted on giving me an extra slab of pecorino for beautiful Francesco who was waiting for me at my apartment.

That night I cut the mozzarella into thick slabs, drizzled it with olive oil, sliced *pomodori* (tomatoes) ripe from the June sun and let the aroma of

tagliatelle ai porcini fill my apartment. I reminisced over the times the doorbell had rung, one by one all my friends entering. Wayne, Michelle, Tommaso, Frances, Jacqui, Karen, Athalee, Attilio, Luigi, Miriam, Roseanne, Rachel, Vanessa, Sarah, Francesco; it seemed like the line would never end. My sisters and their husbands, their children, my brother and my parents completed the scene. Frank Sinatra crooned 'I've got you under my skin' and golden light infused my apartment. The room was filled with the faces that I loved and their laughter and spirited conversation. The scent of slow-baking peaches and coffee beckoned me to the kitchen. I was filled with an indescribable happiness for what my life had become. Outside the lights of Florence twinkled softly. I knew the journey was just beginning, tomorrow would be another adventure and today I am content to have a beautiful black Leica, a tiger-eyed Italian and a table to call my own.

Florence at sunset

me, on the way back from Sicily

I was filled with an indescribable happiness for what my life had

Carla Coulson

become.

Joy
Isabella @ christmas
2007

Grazie

This book (and my new life) was made possible by the outstanding generosity, vision, helping hands and wonderful friendship of the following people.

A giant thank you to Julie Gibbs, Claire de Medici and Sandy Cull for their extraordinary creativity, patience and professionalism with the design, editing and layout. A special thanks to Rachael Oakes Ash for assisting me in every way possible in getting anything and everything published. Annie Williams of Annica in Surry Hills for production of my images. Gianni, Danieli and Sandra from Sky Photographic lab in Florence. Gianluca Maver and Ricardo Mattoni from Print Serve. Federico and staff at Essedi shop who saved me when my computer died on my august deadline. Maresco and Baldo from MB Ottica in Florence. Marta Innocenti Ciulli, Teresa Favi and all the staff at *Collezioni* magazine. Leigh Gazzard for being the world's greatest ex-business partner. Michelè Pero, Sande Kreft, April Haughey, Athalee Brown, Michelle Perrett, Wayne Chick, Frances Martin, Karen Cotton, Caroline Gibbes, Moira Walsh, Amanda Tabberer, Sarah Sclarandis, Roseanne Dowland, Graeme & Treffina Dowland. Dawn Nicholson and Lorna French, The Connigans. Melissa Collison, Adriana Cortazzo, Vicki and David Archer. Pasquale and Antonio, Popi Zazzeri, Monica Sarsini and Ettore Chelazzi, Alessandra 'La Signora'. Michele from Miransu, Vanessa Forbes, Lisa Clifford Consumi, Natasha Bita, Philippa Kundig, Eric Bulson, and all the souls that have I shared dinner with at Popi's table. SGS, Tommy and Sally Tilley.

Tomasso, Attilio Cauli, Rosina Cauli and the Cauli family. Chiara and Guiseppe Cataldi and all of the extended Urbano family. Mariangela Cipriani, Miriam Santarossa, Anico Szabo. Luigi and the boys in the kitchen at Tre Sorelle Positano. Rocco, Sergio Bello and staff at Da Adolfo, Laurito. Tommaso Torniai and Gianpaolo Marchi at Paskowski, Luca Picchi and staff at Rivoire. The ladies in the kitchen and staff at Casalinga Trattoria, Florence. The gorgeous waiters at Florian in Venice. The staff at *Harper's Bazaar*, *Marie Claire* Australia, *Gourmet Traveller*, *Qantas Magazine* and all the other magazines that have assisted me along the way. Miriam, Lorenzo and Pino (his faithful dawg), Silvia Matteoli and the Matteoli family. Marco and Cinzia at Caffe Degli Artigiani. Rosano and father from Nuvoli, Armando and Michele from I Fratellini in Florence and the wonderful staff at Baldovini. Bosco from Arthur's Pizzeria in Paddington. La farmacia di Santa Maria Novella in Florence for generously allowing me to photograph their chapel. My sister Donna McFarlane for her tireless support in dealing with my accounts and any other problem that arises without ever complaining. Steve McFarlane, Jan and Andrew Prichard, Stewart and Cilla Coulson. My nieces and nephews, who star in some of my favourite photos. To Francesco who has carried my bags, pored over my photos for hours, patiently waited with me for the right moment to shoot, and for never complaining or asking me to hurry — my eternal thanks. And to all the people over the years who have generously allowed me to photograph them, I say thanks with all my heart.

LANTERN

Published by the Penguin Group

Penguin Group (Australia), 707 Collins Street, Melbourne, Victoria 3008, Australia (a division of Penguin Australia Pty Ltd)

Penguin Group (USA) Inc., 375 Hudson Street, New York, New York 10014, USA

Penguin Group (Canada), 9 Eglinton Avenue East, Suite 700, Toronto, Ontario, Canada M4V 3B2 (a division of Penguin Canada Books Inc.)

Penguin Books Ltd, 80 Strand, London WC2R 0RL, England

Penguin Ireland, 25 St Stephen's Green, Dublin 2, Ireland (a division of Penguin Books Ltd)

Penguin Books India Pvt Ltd, 11 Community Centre, Panchsheel Park, New Delhi — 110 017, India

Penguin Group (NZ), 67 Apollo Drive, Rosedale, Auckland 0632, New Zealand (a division of Penguin New Zealand Pty Ltd)

Penguin Books (South Africa) (Pty) Ltd, 181 Jan Smuts Avenue, Parktown North, Johannesburg 2196, South Africa

Penguin (Beijing) Ltd, 7F, Tower B, Jiaming Centre, 27 East Third Ring Road North, Chaoyang District, Beijing 100020, China

Penguin Books Ltd, Registered Offices: 80 Strand, London, WC2R 0RL, England

First published by Penguin Group (Australia), a division of Pearson Australia Group Pty Ltd, 2005

10 9 8 7 6 5 4 3 2 1

Design by Sandy Cull © Penguin Group (Australia)

Photography by Carla Coulson

Typeset in Pabst Oldstyle No. 45™ by Midland Typesetters, Maryborough, Victoria and Sandy Cull

Scanning and separations by Splitting Image P/L, Clayton, Victoria

Printed and bound in China by South China Printing Co Ltd

Cataloguing-in-Publication data available from National Library of Australia:

ISBN 978 1 921384 16 5

www.penguin.com.au/lantern